Eddie Van Halen

KNOW THE MAN, PLAY THE MUSIC

Malcolm Dome & Rod Fogg

Eddie Van Halen

Malcolm Dome & Rod Fogg

A BACKBEAT BOOK
First edition 2005
Published by Backbeat Books
600 Harrison Street
San Francisco, CA 94107, US
www.backbeatbooks.com

An imprint of The Music Player Network CMP Media LLC

Published for Backbeat Books by Outline Press Ltd,
2A Union Court, 20-22 Union Road, London SW4 6JP, England
www.backbeatuk.com

ISBN 0-87930-838-9

EDITOR John Morrish
DESIGN Paul Cooper Design

Printed by SNP Excel (China) Company Ltd.

05 06 07 08 09 5 4 3 2 1

CONTENTS

INTRODUCTION

"Eddie Van Halen is my favourite guitarist. He has been for a while. I love the fact that, even when he doesn't realise what he's doing, he still sounds so melodic. Some of the things he does with a guitar are astonishing."

Those are the words of Leslie West of Mountain, a guitar god in his own right and yet someone who believes that Eddie Van Halen is operating in a different dimension to most of his peers. Let's have no doubts, Van Halen reinvigorated the electric guitar at a time when most people believed they'd heard it all. He did it through the simple yet cunning approach of letting his inventive talents take flight, while remaining disciplined and coherent.

The first time most fans heard Eddie's guitar sound was in 1978, when the *Van Halen* album hit the streets. It was a breath of fresh air, a sublime gutter ballet of rich sounds that shivered and shook with the vibrancy of the times. Harj Kallah, a respected London guitar teacher and former touring musician, put the Van Halen style into context:

"Eddie wasn't just a brilliant guitarist, he knew what not to play. It helped that he'd been a drummer, while his brother Alex [the band's drummer] had played guitar – it meant each understood what the other was trying to do. Michael Anthony's bass playing wasn't just solid, it was fluid. And, as a frontman, David Lee Roth had the unusual knack of knowing when to get out of the way of the music and let Eddie have centre stage."

Van Halen were a box of tricks. As a band they were built on the musicianship of Eddie VH, with his unique guitar style, and the ultimate showman, David Lee Roth. The tension, torsion and ties between the pair were to propel the band from the suburbs of Pasadena, California, to the biggest stages in the world. But what also separated the Halens from most others was that they knew how to write songs – when they could be bothered. And here is an interesting fact about the band: in reality, they gave up trying to write consistent, cohesive albums after their second release, the cunningly titled *Van Halen II*. After that, it was all down to a mix of elegant covers, the occasional inspirational moment and a lot of material that was no more than padding designed to cushion any possible commercial freefall. But it worked. The band carried on convincing everyone that they were a valid unit long after the creative juices had started to dry.

Eddie Van Halen shocked and stunned everyone in the late 1970s by daring to be different. His style took inspiration from Jimi Hendrix but also paid more than lip service to the likes of Alan Holdsworth, who, as a jazz/rock performer, never rose above cult status, but who can clearly count the Van Halen man among his devotees. What jazz taught Eddie was the importance of space as much as notes, riffs and melodies. As Richie Sambora of Bon Jovi once remarked: "Sometimes it's what you don't play that says the most about you. Eddie knows this."

Eddie Van Halen never cluttered his sound. It may come across on certain songs as if he's blazing away without a care for the overall impact, but if you listen to the very best of early Van Halen, then you hear a man who can subtly alter mood and timbre. A guitarist who was a pyrotechnician, yet also remarkably deft. And one for whom the concept of space in a song was something to be treasured. This, then, is the story of a great band, fuelled by the musical talents of an all-time great guitarist. It has highs and lows, peaks, troughs and devastation. As in all good human-interest stories, it's the people who ultimately matter. Lights, camera, action…

Eddie Van Halen

A FLYING START

Van Halen's story starts with the brothers themselves: Eddie and Alex. Contrary to public perception, they aren't actually American; the pair are both Dutch, being born within a couple of years of each other in Amsterdam. Alex, born in 1955, is the elder, with Eddie following in 1957. The family – the two brothers and their parents, Eugenia and Jan – relocated to Nijmegen shortly after Eddie's birth. And in 1962 they took the fateful trip that was to change Eddie and Alex's lives: they emigrated to California.

Legend has it that they landed in the States with less than $100, a few suitcases and a piano. The boat journey had taken them nine days. But with a slight name alteration, from the Dutch 'van Halen' to the more American 'Van Halen', the family settled into its new environment. Alex started taking a keen interest in music, and had flamenco guitar lessons. Eddie, meantime, took up the drums.

But then, in a strange quirk, the former lost enthusiasm for the guitar and started to monopolise his younger brother's kit. And when Alex left high school in 1971 to attend Pasadena College, he began to put together bands – lots of them – with strange names like The Broken Combs. Eddie was along for the ride with all of them.

In 1972 the Van Halens formed Mammoth, with Alex on drums, Eddie on guitar/vocals and one Mark Stone on bass. Two years later, they replaced Stone with Michael Anthony, and a truly impressive band began to take shape. The last piece of the jigsaw was the recruitment of a specialist frontman. David Lee Roth was a man from a wealthy Pasadena family who wanted to be Errol Flynn, Elvis, Robert Plant and Bugs Bunny all rolled into one package.

The new high-wire act played anywhere and everywhere, sometimes doing as many as five shows in one night. Like every other group of wannabes playing the famous Sunset Strip in LA, they had to work and get in everyone's face. They had two huge advantages. Firstly, their frontman, David Lee Roth, was excess on legs. He came alive onstage, lived for the spotlight and craved attention. He had personality, the gift of a mouth that ran at the edges, and a line in patter with more froth than a cappuccino machine.

They also had Eddie Van Halen, who immediately captured the imagination of musicians everywhere with his unique sound and style. He had elements of metal, jazz and rock'n'roll, but was offering something new. He wasn't tied to the past like so many. His sound was flamboyant yet understated, effusive yet introspective. He could make the guitar sing, but he could also make it sound menacing.

The band worked up a set of strong songs and, after a few false starts, landed the all-important record deal, their gateway to the stars and beyond.

Nobody outside of California had a clue who this band were, but all that was about to change. Warner Brothers won the race to sign Van Halen, and set about trying to turn their obvious potential into something commercially viable. They chose in-house producer Ted

Templeman to work with the band, a relationship that was to prove long and fruitful. Van Halen also had one not so obvious advantage…

Just a few years previously, the same label had signed Montrose, one of the most exciting young hard rock bands in America. Their self-titled debut, produced by Templeman, was to be hailed as a bona fide classic. But it took 11 years for it to reach even the gold standard in America, which is 500,000 copies sold. The singer in the band at the time, Sammy Hagar (who was to become associated with Van Halen in the mid-1980s), had a theory about all of this: "When Warners signed Montrose they had very little experience in dealing with our sort of music. They made a lot of mistakes both in the production of the record and also its marketing. But they learned from this, and Van Halen reaped the benefit. In a way, they couldn't have signed to the label at a better time."

The band's debut album, *Van Halen*, shocked the rock world. Why? Because it was different. With most of the media and the music industry obsessed with punk and new wave, the whole metal and hard rock community was on its uppers. The reason was plain to see: most of the giants of the genre had become dinosaurs, no longer capable of connecting with the new generation of fans, who wanted their own heroes, not hand-me-downs from elder siblings.

So the stage was set for Van Halen to capture the imagination – and they had what it took. They had a frontman who oozed cool and charisma with a whiff of decadence, a guitarist who was the first true guitar hero for the modern age and songs that dripped with spontaneity but also melody. It all added up to a band going places, ready to convince the world they were reinventing the wheel.

Van Halen opens with an ear-catching, inspired moment: a backwards car horn sound that leads into an ominous bass line. The car horn effect had first been suggested by Gene Simmons of Kiss. He'd worked previously with the band on a demo (three tracks) and had used the sound sample to end a song. Sadly, Simmons couldn't persuade any label to take the demo seriously, and bowed out of the picture prior to the Warners deal. But his production input was put to good use, as the band took the car horn sound and placed it at the start of 'Runnin' With The Devil'.

But having got people's attention with this unusual start, the band then opened up the song with Eddie's guitar style, which immediately seemed to be operating at a higher level than anything anyone had heard for years. It was majestic, flamboyant, tight, opinionated and focused. And as his hands flashed across the strings, there was a resounding resonance – this was the devil's music, and he had new pals. When Roth sang "I live my life like there's no tomorrow", he was sounding both the ethos of band and their philosophy – one that everyone who listened appreciated and aspired towards. Van Halen's solo again is unusual because it always seems to remain on the surface, never attacking. Others would have been over-emphatic but Eddie gets the maximum impact through minimal force and great technique. 'Runnin' With The Devil' set the tone, scene and purpose for the album. It's one of the all-time great opening tracks and remains as powerful today as it did when first heard.

'Jamie's Cryin'' again uses limited force, relying more on ingenuity than pace or aggression. This isn't a power ballad, but is certainly taken at a sedate velocity. However, Eddie Van Halen's guitar is almost solely responsible for giving the song a slightly sinister feel. It's uncomfortable at times, as Eddie explores the range of his abilities. To call this genius might be overstating the case, but it certainly goes against the good-time grain of this incarnation of the band.

'Ain't Talkin' 'Bout Love' is one of the most poignant songs Van Halen ever recorded. From the sedate charm of Eddie's guitar intro through to the middle section, with Roth crooning about how he's "Been to the edge and tried to look down/You know I've lost a lot of friends that way", this is an unusual song, built on a guitar structure that seems spartan and sparse compared to the overblown approach most musicians would have taken. Eddie Van Halen showed something of a swooping, crash-and-burn, incendiary attitude, yet was also a technician of the highest value. His guitar, covered with tape, looked as if it had been made from old pieces of wood lying around desperate for a reason to exist. This wasn't the reality, of course, but it was all part of a carefully constructed Van Halen myth, which we'll consider in a short while.

> Eddie's guitar, covered in black tape, looked as if it had been made from old pieces of wood lying around.

Back on *Van Halen*, the flow of songs never abates. 'Atomic Punk' has little to do with Johnny Rotten, and is more of a futuristic streetwise strut, again with Roth affecting what was to become a characteristic snigger as he claims, "Nobody walks these streets at night, except me."

There isn't a bad moment here, but there are two outstanding pieces of music, outrageous in their impact. 'Eruption' is an Eddie Van Halen solo, just him and his guitar, flailing through the whole gamut of bombast and blast in 102 seconds. This is a fierce, combative, challenging solo that growls, snarls and bites deep. It's a tireless tribute to the Van Halen style that would set the tone with guitarists for a decade. In a way, it's surprising to hear something like this on an album, but the band were fully aware that they had to exploit the obvious originality of their star musician. And it had the desired effect, as people raved about the hottest guitarist America had produced since ... well, Jimi Hendrix.

The other master track is a cover of The Kinks' 'You Really Got Me'. Now, if we are to search for the roots of heavy metal then here they are, in the song that is most recognisable from this distance as the oldest metal tune. In every respect, it is the birth of the genre we know and love. But in 1978, how many people remembered The Kinks? Van Halen again brought it to everyone's attention, doing such a good job that many didn't realise it was a cover.

Eddie Van Halen updated Dave Davies' early 1960s guitar sound, but never lost the matador feel of the original. Listen to the opening chords, as

THE HOTTEST GUITARIST AMERICA HAD PRODUCED SINCE JIMI HENDRIX

Eddie hits the strings and delivers a stirring juxtaposition between the demands of 1978 and the requirement for nostalgic interpretation. And it's also on this song that singer and guitarist work best; you really can hear a special rapport between the pair. Roth occasionally mimics Van Halen's guitar, which in turn affectionately mocks his vocal scats. Breathtaking.

Covers were to play a crucial role in Van Halen's early career; they also covered 'Ice Cream Man', by Chicago bluesman John Brim, who died in 2003 at the age of 81. This allowed the Vegas tendencies of the band to shine through. While retaining the blues essence of the original, they gave it some gloss and sheen, and also a real edge, crashing it headlong into a roulette table at the sleaziest casino in town. It worked, but then Van Halen – for all their annoying inconsistencies – were always able to take other people's songs and give them their own spin to great effect.

Van Halen was released to an overload of critical acclaim and near hysteria from a fresh generation of rock fans who had found their own heroes. Unlike the punk movement, Van Halen had no interest in sweeping away the old guard – they just wanted to take over from them. And with one of the great debut albums, they did just that.

It was trashy, sleazy, at times even sloppy, but the record was exciting. It also had the extra dimension of sounding as if it was born out of a jam session in the studio – the foursome had truly hit the ground running. Is it an overrated album? Not at all. *Van Halen* is a masterpiece, so right for its time, and still sounding as vibrant as ever. In many respects, it defined the band's career, but it also became a millstone. They were never to top it.

On the road, the band proved the equal of the record. They had the confidence, zest and youthful arrogance to tour with Black Sabbath and give the British metal legends a bloodied nose every night. Who will ever forget the performance in London, when Van Halen tore the place apart and made the headliners seem tired, listless and outmoded. Eddie Van Halen versus Tony Iommi? No contest. The former was the new star in the firmament, with the technique, power and stature required to stamp himself as the most important guitarist of his generation.

It was the birth of a legend – but in some ways it was the conclusion as well.

RUSHED INTO THE STUDIO

By the end of the world tour to support and promote their debut album, Van Halen were the template for a new era in American hard rock/metal. They were the benchmark by which all others would be judged. They were heroes – and none more so than their guitarist. Eddie Van Halen's technique had turned the globe on its head. Everyone wanted to copy him, work out his style and become a disciple of a man who was taking the guitar into fresh arenas. He was the master, the natural successor to Hendrix. What next for him? And what next for a band who would surely dominate the 1980s?

David Lee Roth, meanwhile, was very much the ringmaster. His energy and vivacity onstage won over even the most sceptical audience, thereby allowing his bandmates to concentrate on the music. In some ways, Roth took the heat for the others. But slowly he was starting to dominate, and this wasn't necessarily for the good of the band.

Behind the scenes, the singer was taking a more active role in the business area. Van Halen were now big moneyspinners and Roth was determined to ensure that the band got their due all the way down the line.

But while they'd made such a huge impact with *Van Halen*, the band were never to fulfil that potential. They often struggled against their own talent and ambition. In the Roth era, they seemed to become rather lazy in the studio, settling for a series of albums containing substandard material, with only the odd bright spark to light things up. What caused this approach? A series of circumstances seemed to conspire against Van Halen ever reaping the artistic rewards that were theirs for the taking.

But despite this constant failure to live up to expectations, the myth and legend of Van Halen just grew. Every album that came out after *Van Halen* was met with a chorus of confusion, followed by adulation that seemed misguided yet unstoppable. The myth of Van Halen? Indeed, one built on the guitar work of one of the Van Halen brothers, plus the hyperdriven, warp-factor-six mouth of David Lee Roth, a man schooled in soundbites and in providing enough verbal nonsense, punctuated with outbursts of laughter, to deflect any difficult question. He spoke in aphorisms and metaphors. If you actually read any interview he gave, you will notice he rarely answered awkward questions.

But did anyone care? Not really. This was entertainment. Van Halen were in the business of making sure people left the venues with smiles on their faces, having of course spent a small fortune on merchandise. But little of their energy seemed to go into the studio with them; they made album after album that mostly sounded bored.

Van Halen II – the title gave away the problem – came out in 1979, to much head-scratching and disappointment. It was clear the band weren't too sure where they should be heading. They were still intense and passionate, but what for? On first listen, one hears the band caught between stools: they weren't as sensational and exciting as on the first record, because everyone had heard all of that before. It wasn't new. But to move on would have meant taking too much of a risk. Change and you might lose a fan base that had only just been built. So, with that slightly confused and confusing approach, the band had gone back into the studio with Ted Templeman and delivered … not a great deal.

The whole project was too rushed, and it's clear on the understated opening song that the band aren't all pulling in the same direction. The first song is a cover of Russ Ballard's 'You're No Good', originally done by Linda Ronstadt. For a player of world-class talent, Eddie Van Halen's performance here is woeful. Lazy, lacking and lacklustre, it's as if he doesn't want to know. There something so mediocre about it all that one had to wonder whether this was indeed the same person who, a year previously, had set the world on fire. The new age hero was already losing his lustre. Add to this the fact that David Lee Roth's vocals are about as shiny and bright as a sack of coal, and you have the worst cover Van Halen ever attempted.

After such an opening, things could only improve – surely! They did. 'Dance The Night Away' would be their first US Top 20 hit and it had more brio and brushstrokes than 'You're No Good'. Eddie's playing is once again back on track, as he combines lighting flashes with more steady storms. This is what people wanted from him – even though, at times it does sound as if he threw in one of the guitar limbo dances that were now becoming his trademark just so everyone knew it was him. Over-elaboration is understandable, though.

The band were also capable of some truly heavy moments. 'Somebody Get Me A Doctor' and 'Light Up The Sky' rely on the Alex Van Halen/Michael Anthony partnership to whip up the rhythmic gravy, while Eddie bends the strings in a fashion that proves that, when he wanted to, there were few anywhere in the world who could match his versatility or depth of performance. It's almost cathartic, as he provides covering fire for David Lee Roth.

'Spanish Fly' also works here, being a more gentle acoustic work-out. Let's give the band credit, they never sound straitjacketed into the acoustic environment; it's all so natural, with Eddie once again triumphant in a change of style and pace. It's with moments like these that Eddie actually proved his genius.

However, the overall impact of the album was a lot less than that of *Van Halen*. With hindsight, the band were rushed into the studio too soon after coming off the road. They should have taken their time, soaked up the success they'd enjoyed, put it into the context of their

David Lee Roth was the ringmaster on stage. His energy and vivacity soon won over the most difficult audience.

own lives and then, more balanced and prepared, done a record that moved the Van Halen story forward. Instead, they were stuck with a patchwork record that was neither natural successor to *Van Halen*, nor a dramatic move forward. And was there already dissent in the camp?

If you listen carefully to the abum you can actually hear some irritation in the playing and performance. Whereas on the first record the harmony between 'Diamond Dave' and Eddie Van Halen was palpable, here there are times when the pair seem out of sync. One must ask if this was deliberate or sub-conscious, and whether Templeman went along with it.

This is hardly something new between a singer and guitarist. The dynamic tension has been part of almost every great band – it helps drive them forward. But here it was more negative. Dave Roth was trying to introduce a more Vegas style of rock'n'roll to the proceedings, while Eddie wanted to take more musical risks – to do anything less would bore both of them.

We are talking about two restive spirits, who had vision and could taste success, but each saw a different path to his particular Nirvana. To keep ahead of the pack who would come gnawing at their feet, Van Halen couldn't afford to stand still. They'd inspired a new generation to pick up guitars and ride towards the sound of the guns. Now those acolytes were aiming to shoot down the masters. Old tricks would have to be revamped, and new ones brought in. The challenge was there, but could this band rise to it? They'd gone in the space of a year from the hottest young band on the planet to superstars who were already running out of track as their train went loco. Everywhere they went, Van Halen were conquering heroes, and the demand for yet more shone through the eyes of every fan they encountered. They were being bled dry by the most vampiric force in rock – devotion.

> VAN HALEN HAD INSPIRED A NEW GENERATION. THE CHALLENGE WAS THERE, BUT COULD THIS BAND RISE TO IT?

They got through this period through a combination of energy, momentum, drink and substances – the usual rock'n'roll diet. But to step into the new decade still being hailed as the leaders of the pack they needed to move forward and move on. The partying was out of control, yet the two men who were the twin pillars of the band's future were still capable of focusing on what was required and making it happen. Dave Roth and Eddie Van Halen just needed to realise how much each gives to the other and how much they needed to get the best from themselves.

David Lee Roth was, is, and always will be a highly competitive man. He wants to get to the top wherever he is, whatever he's doing. The success Van Halen had so far achieved had merely whetted his appetite. Now he wanted to march into the new decade and dominate it. To this end he needed a guitarist prepared again to run risks and dig deep. But would he get it? Would Van Halen fans get it?

FINDING THE FORMULA

By 1980, and the birth of the new decade, Van Halen were heroes. They had so successfully reinvented the concept of American heavy metal that most people had come to regard them as *the* state-of-the-art troupe. By any known definition, they were megastars, outstripping most bands when it came to excess and commercial power. Eddie Van Halen had retooled guitar technique to such an extent that the flamboyance of his delivery, coupled to the sheer bravura of the attack, made him the inspiration for many aspiring guitarists. He was, however, about to be supplanted by Randy Rhoads, an unknown young American who had been handpicked to help revitalize Ozzy Osbourne's career as he took his first post-Sabbath steps into a hostile world.

But back in the Van Halen camp, there were intriguing stirrings. Having now conquered the world more than once – and proven they were in this for the long haul – the band seemed to take their collective foot off the pedal. They now embarked on a part of their career when minimum effort was applied to achieve the maximum result. The band were almost delirious in finding a formula in the studio that allowed them to confuse and confound the fans and the media.

By this time Van Halen's music was starting to become a little more challenging. Yet they also had a sensibility that wanted to spend as little time as possible in the studio. They determined – correctly – that as long as they had a couple of winning songs per record, the rest could be filler material and the fans would still buy the results. It was a cynical ploy. But such was their influence and reputation, as a band challenging the boundaries, that they not only got away with this but emerged triumphant.

The first record to really showcase this approach was 1980's *Women And Children First*. It opens well enough, with the jungle rhythms and mantra of 'And The Cradle Will Rock', which allows David Lee Roth almost to scat his way through a song that really did lock into the sensibility of the streets. "Well, they say it's kinda fright'nin' how this younger generation swings. You know, it's more than just some new sensation," he smirks, getting right to the heart of the matter, about the divide between the generations, about how teenagers will always find some way to rebel. But the song gets a little darker when Roth talks about kids ending up on the street, "Tied to whoever they meet." There's an element of desperation here that is out of step with the usual Van Halen good time outlook. This is accentuated by some of the most fascinating guitar work ever produced by Eddie Van Halen.

Listen to the almost understated, percusive intro to the song, as the band's rhythm section locks into a stride that may not be rap, but has elements of what makes that genre work: the pulse is definitely gangland, establishing something steamy and seamy. This is not wholesome music at all, and riding over the top of everything comes Eddie's guitar. Acting almost as a guide to the netherworld, it is one of the best performances the man has ever given, swooping, snarling and snatching at chords in a fashion that again showed he could be highly inventive when the occasion demanded. In many respects, while he didn't detune for the song, Eddie did point his guitar in this direction. And perhaps this can be construed as a template for so much that has happened with rock and metal guitar over the past decade or so. What's more, this was the first Van Halen song to carry keyboards, albeit processed through a guitar amp to provide a heavier, thicker sound.

This was the obvious highlight on the record. There were precious few others. 'Everybody Wants Some!' could have been written for either of the first two albums, such is its glitzy pop attitude, but there's something altogether tired and bored about the whole structure. It goes on too long, and no member of the band appears to be up for the task in hand. They all sound rather indifferent to the fate of the tune. Everybody might want some, but would they be prepared to accept something that's so obviously mediocre? The answer seem to be 'Yes', because the record came out to positive reviews and high sales. What might also have helped was the simplistic, bluesy 'Could This Be Magic?', which in many ways pointed to a future when the band would content themselves with a straightforward pop-rock approach – but that would only happen once Dave Roth had elected to move on.

The album cover for *Women And Chldren First* showed the four members of the band almost falling over each other in their

> Thanks to the over-size personality of David Lee Roth, Van Halen were stronger than ever as a live attraction.

bonhomie. Whereas the first record had gone for individual studio shots of the band, and the second one had come out with just the by-now famous Van Halen logo, this time around they seemed determined to show they were a gang, all pals together. It's a stylish, cool and significant photo – the only time the band as a whole would appear on an album cover during the David Lee Roth era – and the photo was so good it was an art work in its own right. The man behind the album sleeve concept and design was someone who'd been with the band for a while: Pete Angelus. He was starting to make his presence felt in terms of the artistic creativity that was to be so much a part of the Van Halen process. And when the split happened with Dave Roth, he was to become Roth's business partner.

The release of *Women And Children First* came in a significant year for hard rock and heavy metal. It was the year when AC/DC released *Back In Black,* with new singer Brian Johnson, to huge acclaim. It was the year when Black Sabbath replaced Ozzy with Ronnie James Dio and recorded the landmark *Heaven & Hell* album. It was the year when the New Wave Of British Heavy Metal came into its own, when Iron Maiden issued their self-titled debut, Saxon gave the world *Wheels Of Steel* and *Strong Arm Of The Law*, and Def Leppard rode *On Through The Night*. It was the year of Motorhead's *Ace Of Spades*, Ozzy's *Blizzard Of Ozz* and Judas Priest's *British Steel*. It was the year of the first Castle Donington Monsters Of Rock Festival in the UK (with Rainbow headlining). Up against such significance, Van Halen's contribution now seems somewhat pallid. But their momentum hardly faltered.

What still set the band apart from so many was that they'd become cultural icons. Thanks to the personable and personality-driven David Lee Roth, Van Halen were stronger than ever when they hit the road. And they were also making more obvious financially orientated

> ## VAN HALEN'S SOUND WAS BECOMING MORE COMPLEX, AS EDDIE EXPLORED SYNTHS AND KEYBOARDS

decisions. For instance, whereas the UK and Europe had been a significant part of the band's touring schedule up until now, fans on that side of the world weren't to get another chance to see their heroes up close until 1984. But live, the band were better than they'd ever been. The stage set was becoming bigger as their fame demanded they play bigger venues in America.

Dave Roth's personality was also growing. He was becoming the consummate frontman, combining sexuality, athleticism, dance routines, comedic touches and the demeanour of a TV game show host. Here was someone who gave his all onstage, whilst seemingly turning his back on the studio. But Van Halen's sound was was now more complex than before, with a greater number of layers, due, in part, to the fact that Eddie wanted to explore the potential of synthesizers and keyboards. So, here was another problem within the Van Halen camp: could they possibly equate Roth's demand for ever more ludicrous stage presentations, with the more musically cohesive and diverse needs of the rest of the band? It led to conflict between the various parties behind the scenes, and sowed the seeds for the discontent that would lead to the departure of Roth in 1984, just as the band were reaching the height of their career. But all of that was to come. For the moment, Van Halen were seemingly unstoppable.

TENSION IN THE CAMP

After *Women And Children First* had been released, Van Halen took a brief break to celebrate a major occasion in Eddie Van Halen's life: he married girlfriend Valerie Bertinelli in April 1981.

The pair had met backstage after a Van Halen show in Shreveport, Louisiana. At the time, Bertinelli was just 20, but already a major TV star, thanks to a sitcom called *One Day At A Time*. Van Halen producer Ted Templeman put it this way:

"The moment they laid eyes on each other, it was like, 'Aw, man, forget it.' There was a lot of pressure on him by the band not to marry her, but I think they were meant for each other."

It must be said that, rather than encouraging the romance, the rest of the band did indeed try to drive a wedge between the couple. To them, the marriage represented a sign that at least one of their company was ready to grow up, become an adult and accept the responsibilities of life. Yet on stage they were still the ultimate rock'n'roll party band. The two lifestyles couldn't be equated, at least in the minds of Eddie's brother Alex, Michael Anthony and Dave Roth. So the wedding, when it happened, wasn't the cause of anything like the wild celebrations it should have been. Eddie, to some extent, was now apart from his bandmates. The gang was over. Time to go home?

Things got so bad that, in an effort to keep Valerie away from Eddie while the band toured, Roth banned all girlfriends from coming backstage. Partly this was to protect their decadent and notorious approach to touring – none more hedonistic – but there was also an element of control in Roth's attitude. Trying to separate the band members from anyone who could exert an outside influence was his way of maintaining the status quo that had served the band so well. The arrival of long-term girlfriends and wives seemed to threaten what had made the band happen in the first place.

Roth might have been a little unfair in his approach, but it also must be said he alone understood that Van Halen couldn't just play at being the ultimate party combo – they had to live what they preached. For David Lee Roth this was an adventure – nothing was taboo, everything should be sampled, expect that which takes away from the essence of what makes the scene swing. However, he was losing the battle with Eddie. The guitarist and his wife would spend many a night huddled together in the tuning room on tour, trying to get some peace and quiet, away from the madness, mayhem and mania. It was something of a miserable existence for the couple, and for the rest of the band as well. Surely, things couldn't be allowed to go on that way?

The next sign of a genuine rift within the camp came with the new album, *Fair Warning*, which, like *Women And Children First*, offered the occasional gem, and much treading of the proverbial water. Again, Templeman was in charge, and once more one gets the distinct feeling that the band desperately needed something else, somebody else, to kick them hard. They were too comfortable with the set-up, too ingrained in a way of working that, to be brutal, no longer worked. It's hard to appreciate what it must have been like for Van Halen at this juncture. They were the ultimate American hard rock band, living a dream that was turning into a nightmare – or at least turning sour. Without the gang spirit that had fuelled their rise to the top, *Fair Warning* was a little depressing. The good times were no longer at all obvious – or at least couldn't be sustained for long enough. To say that Van Halen were in a state of disarray is an exaggeration, but they certainly seemed to be struggling to find a way into a fresh era.

Musically they'd already defined themselves and set the standards. Now they were in desperate need of a new challenge. They'd become too comfortable, which was anathema for both the singer and the guitarist. Here were a pair of creative artists who craved constant threats and experimentation. They couldn't just maintain the status quo, because their very spirit and nature couldn't allow it. And yet, here were Van Halen in 1981 doing precisely that. It is no wonder that there was dissent and tension within the camp.

For Eddie, particularly, there seemed to be no way forward. He had practically re-invented the concept of rock guitar just a few years earlier, introducing classical scales into a medium hitherto dominated by blues influences. He had inspired people to pick up a guitar like nobody since Hendrix. He had taken the instrument forward into a new era – and possibly saved the concept of the guitar hero. But what now?

David Lee Roth found solace and outlets for his boundless energy elsewhere. Constantly restive and restless, he took up mountaineering and other pursuits that challenged his psyche and mental strength. Seemingly no longer able to get his rocks off solely by being onstage, this intelligent, robust man was now seeking thrills elsewhere outside of rock'n'roll – and they were far from cheap.

As for Alex Van Halen and Michael Anthony, they seemed to be caught in the middle of a furious battle between the two high-profile high-kickers in the band, forever waiting in the background for everything to come together again. Would *Fair Warning* find the band able to regroup, realign and push the boundaries once again? Or were we to witness yet another jumble of confusion, confounding the four members of the band rather more than it did the media or the fans? Van Halen desperately needed to find a way to go forward, to satisfy the creative lusts of their two protagonists. And they needed the drive and cohesion to come from elsewhere. It didn't.

The *Fair Warning* album was again a mess, occasionally providing evidence of the spark and sparkle that had first lifted the band to undreamt heights, but for the most part lacking in the precision and motivation that had sent *Van Halen* spinning on a journey into greatness. Here was an obviously brilliant band, still capable of matchless wit and wisdom, once more content to work well below their capacity. Whatever determination, passion and focus the band had taken with them into the studio soon dissipated as they failed to capture what was required.

Not that the album is a complete failure: with a band this talented, there are inevitably moments when the full strengths of the individuals collide to the benefit of the music. 'Mean

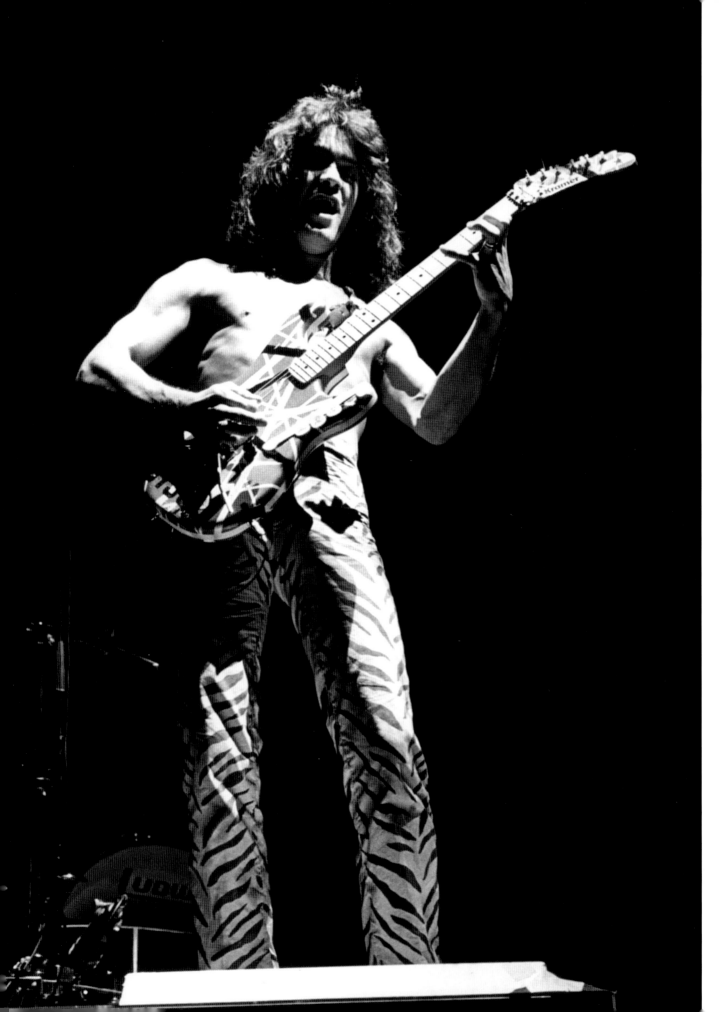

Street' is a fine first salvo – possible the best opening cut they'd managed since 'Runnin' With The Devil'. Eddie finds his range and target easily here, heading into the song with a flurry of near frustration. It's as if he's telling the rest of the band that he can play this sort of neo-classical, effect-laden burst forever if that's what they want – but there's so much more he wants to do. It's a cry for help, as well as being one of the best guitar-orientated intros in hard rock. It's belligerent, bellicose, full of brio and bravura, and seemingly has the man playing as if his life depended on it. But was anyone listening to the inner voice that fuelled the outburst?

The intro itself doesn't lead into a bombastic riot of sound and colour, as might have been expected. Despite the intro and the title, the song itself is built on a funky groove that suits the band perfectly. It struts its stuff with a pimp's fashion sense. There's a swagger to the music that is joyous, and once the song settles – or rather unsettles – down, the band get into a groove that works because it's uneasy. At any moment you expect Eddie to hit a time change, a different key, to disrupt the harmony. He never does, but every time you hear the song, the expectation is never far from the surface.

The only spellbinding track here is 'Unchained', which has a more typical Van Halen hard rock flourish. It opens with a rousing riff from Eddie, again giving the impression of a man trying to break out of his self-imposed prison and go for something a little different. It's headbanging music. It's almost acoustic, yet also so reliant on the chord structure that gets a body gyrating. It is a masterstroke, and remains one of the band's finest achievements. Once the song bursts into life, again you are floored by the power and fascination of the foursome. This is a song about freedom, about ridding yourself of the chains of life and … well, having a good time. "Hit the ground running," smirks Roth, more as a matter of course than anything else. This is the story of Van Halen up until that point, captured in words and music. Few bands had ever broken the shackles so completely and hit the ground running with such conviction.

And yet, it was the act of breaking free of the usual musical shackles that now put

> **EDDIE SOUNDS LIKE A MAN TRYING TO BREAK OUT OF A SELF-IMPOSED PRISON**

Van Halen into a straitjacket of their own choosing. When all restrictions have gone, how do you discipline your career, your dreams?

The rest of *Fair Warning* really does underline the band's problems. It desperately searches for a reason to exist. Whether going for red-faced rockers, or laying back just a little, Van Halen just cannot seem to get into top gear. All the problems that were staring to become crucial beneath the surface were affecting their music. They could no longer hide the rifts. Listening to *Fair Warning* makes it obvious – this was no longer a happy band of brothers pulling in the same direction. The sheer force of will that determined the early success of Van Halen was now no more than a charade. And yet it was a myth everyone still wanted to buy into.

The strange thing about Van Halen is that they'd so completely won over the public with that combination of musical genius and wit, they could do anything they wished and get away with it – just. But sub-standard songs like 'Dirty Movies' and 'Sinners Swing!' were eroding the confidence and commitment of even the diehards. Sales figures for albums were starting to peak and fans would still turn out in their thousands for shows – because it was here the band still shone. But *Fair Warning* proved that something radical was needed if the band were not to be buried under an avalanche of new talent, inspired by the Halens, yet ready to take their place. The leadership of this band had to be grasped and guided.

At this point, they still had two masters – Eddie Van Halen and David Lee Roth – and, while the latter was winning the battle for the hearts and minds of the fans and enforcing his will on the band, was he actually taking them forward? Eddie, meanwhile, was desperate for Van Halen to get back to their roots and rediscover a joy in taking musical risks and exploring fresh dimensions. With a singer who was seemingly more in tune with Vegas lounge suits and glitter, and a record company that demanded consistent sales figures, the very fibre of the band – something Eddie understood all too well – was being ripped apart. He was trapped. Was there any way forward? Maybe he started to contemplate life without Dave Roth, possibly without the band. But worse was to come.

A WHOLE NEW MARKET

By the start of 1982, eccentricity had begun to take hold of the Van Halen camp. And 'camp' was the operative word. David Lee Roth was starting to establish an outrageous mode of behaviour that was certainly eye-catching: he would constantly patrol the backstage areas and also the party zones in the company of an unusual gang of 'security' dwarves. Most of this was to make an impact; whether they'd have been any use in a difficult situation remains open to speculation. But it was a typical Roth move – always looking for some way to upstage anyone and everyone.

'Diamond Dave' was – still is – a complex soul. But unlike many multi-faceted personalities who aren't particularly adept at adapting to specific situations, Dave has always been a master of the craft. He can turn on the charm. He can be ruthless. He can be the party. He can also be introspective.

Two things drive David Lee Roth forward. One is competitiveness; the other is a formidable insecurity. Both manifest themselves in a public display of confidence that sometimes borders on the insufferable. Dave has never walked into a room; he demands to be the centre of attention, sweeping all before him. His is a personality that refuses to be denied or subdued. It's what has made him one of the greatest live performers in rock history. It's what played a key role in establishing Van Halen as a great live act, whatever their studio deficiencies.

But it was also putting the two halves of the band on a collision course, with the inevitable outcome that the town wouldn't be big enough for Diamond Dave and Eddie VH, the golden boy of the guitar.

While the band cooled their heels after the lengthy *Fair Warning* tour, Eddie accepted an interesting offer. Michael Jackson was working on an album called *Thriller*, and Eddie was asked to contribute his inimitable guitar style to one of the songs on that record, namely 'Beat It'. According to Toto's Steve Lukather, who was also involved with the project, this is how Van Halen's guitar part was cut: "Quincy Jones [the producer] and Michael took a skeleton version of the song up to Eddie Van Halen's place, as they wanted him to solo over the verse section. However, he played over a section that had more chord changes. So to fit his solo to where it went in the song, they had to cut the tape, which took a lot of time to synchronise together.

"After they had managed this, [Toto drummer] Jeff Porcaro and me were called in to bind Eddie's solo and some haphazard percussion, which was a major headache. Initially, we rocked it out as Eddie had played a good solo, but Quincy thought it too tough. So I had to reduce the distorted guitar sound and this is what was released. It was a huge R&B/rock success for us all really and helped pave the way for the bands of today that fuse these styles."

Eddie Van Halen's guitar part on 'Beat It' was an important part of the song, leading the whole number into an area that had been out of bounds as far as the pop mainstream was concerned. The fusion of R&B and hard rock was different – even a little bizarre. But it worked brilliantly on all fronts. For Michael Jackson, it gained him an immediate entree into the world of rock music, and Van Halen fans were guaranteed to check out the performance of their hero, thereby opening up a whole new market to a man who was already dominant in his own sphere. This clever piece of realignment played a major role in developing *Thriller* into the biggest selling record of all time.

So, what did Eddie get out of it himself? Financially, not as much as he might. He didn't have a royalty deal. "I did it as a favour," he said in 1984. "I didn't want anything. Maybe Michael will give me dance lessons someday. I was a complete fool, according to the rest of Van Halen, our manager and everybody else. I was not used. I knew what I was doing. I don't do something unless I want to do it."

And let's put another perspective on what the guitarist got out of this alliance. He had been struggling for a couple of years to get the rest of his band to stretch out, take risks and push the proverbial envelope. It seemed to be all in vain. Whatever he said, however much he questioned where the band was going, nothing seemed to change the course and path. They were simply heading towards another excursion to the studio that would once again prove dull and rather lame as far as Eddie was concerned.

Where was the dynamism, the freshness, the challenge? How strange that the guitarist found solace and a chance to go for it with someone like Michael Jackson, a man who had little to do with his world. But Eddie's guitar performance on 'Beat It' was one of his most inspired in years. It wasn't particularly different – that wasn't why he was chosen – but he sounds as if he's rising to a fresh set of challenges. Eddie Van Halen knows he's doing something here that could prove to be historic. He was helping to fuse two disparate genres, ones that had once been a lot closer, but had drifted apart, and were now separated by a mental chasm. Yet, the impact of 'Beat It' – which was to be one of many singles from the *Thriller* album – was to be far-reaching. It showed what could be done, it displayed a courage that could have easily backfired and alienated both R&B and rock fans. Of course, history proves that it did not – it opened up the possibilities, and laid a foundation for what was to happen several years later, when crossing the genre divide suddenly became the thing to do. The question for Eddie was now: could he persuade his VH cohorts to take a similar risk?

The *Diver Down* album is arguably the strangest of Van Halen's career. Depending on your viewpoint, it's either a disaster or a triumph. Half of the album features covers and there are also three comparatively short instrumentals. As the whole album barely lasts 30 minutes, one could argue that this is the most appalling moment in VH history until that moment. And yet, the band really did seem to have recaptured their joie de vivre again. They really were on fire, and having fun. Did anyone care that there were five covers here? Did anyone really sit down with a stopwatch and time the whole thing? That was never the Van Halen attitude. Never mind the quantity, just sit back, light up a fat one, grab a beer and a friend and just have some fun tonight.

Exactly what persuaded the band to go for this oddball direction remains open to conjecture. The probability is that so many covers were necessary because they simply couldn't come up with enough new material to make the whole thing work. But it was something of an inspired move, albeit one that confounded everyone.

The opening cover proved to be a return visit to the Kinks' back catalogue – something Van Halen did with considerable success, of course, on their first album with 'You Really Got Me'. Now they went for the slightly more obscure 'Where Have All The Good Times Gone', which might have been cunningly chosen by Van Halen, because that's the way they felt. Whatever the sentiments, the delivery is precise, straight on the mark and puts a knuckleduster between the eyes. This was Van Halen back on the mark, locking together in a way they'd rarely done since their debut four years previously. Eddie's guitar playing is back to its sharpest and meanest as he cuts out the flab and goes for a sound that once more puts him ahead of the pack. If anything, he's understating as well. No histrionics here to get noticed, but an air of relaxation not heard for a while.

'Hang 'Em High' is one of the few originals here. Based around a blistering Eddie Van Halen solo – exactly what fans wanted from the man – it's a heavy, almost piledriving number that catches a whiff of the metal explosion then sweeping the rock world. For once, the band go for the kill and take no prisoners. All too often Van Halen had threatened to explode on a song, only to take out their tickling stick. This time there was to be no messing – and Eddie saw to it that the track stayed on course.

'Cathedral' is a vignette, a short instrumental interlude and a chance to catch your breath. But again it depends on Eddie's ingenuity as he uses a delay effect to augment a strange guitar sound. It works rather well, and acts as the perfect complement to what's already been heard and what's about to hit the listener. So 'Cathedral' serves two purposes: as a linking moment, and also as a track in its own right.

Next comes the rather ambient, laid-back, formulaic 'Secrets'. This is really a vocal showcase, as Dave Roth gets the opportunity to shine through, and prove he can carry a tune, despite the misgivings of many. And if you listen to the backing vocals, from Michael Anthony, it's easy to see why many believe he actually has a better voice than the man out front. Eddie's guitar is restrained here; he's no need to show off his skills or make his mark. To do so would have been to undermine the song itself, and that was never his way.

'Intruder' is again a short instrumental, nothing particularly innovative or stunning about it, but again it acts as a bridge, this time between 'Secrets' and arguably the album's outstanding track, a superb cover of the Roy Orbison song '(Oh) Pretty Woman'. While many may claim that 'You Really Got Me' was the band's finest cover, this one shades it for others. It is just tailor-made for Van Halen. The strut, the dream, the chat, it's all here, as Roth and Eddie Van Halen combine in a way they'd hardly done for years. Eddie seems to relish the opportunity to get to grips with a bona fide classic and remake it in his own image. His guitar work has the funky stride of a jive-talking dude. Whilst never toppling over into soul or R&B, it does give the whole song a pace and purpose that owes much to black rhythms. This is among the best playing of Eddie's career.

David Lee Roth inevitably relishes the lyrics, caressing each syllable like he's planning a seduction. This is a master class from one of the great vocalists in how to combine sensuality and dirty inference while making the whole damn thing sound like it's never been attempted before. Oh, and this was the biggest hit of the band's career to date in America.

Following on from this wonderful exposition of the art of the cover version, the band take a trip in a more soulful direction with a version of Martha Reeves & The Vandellas' 'Dancing In The Street', later to be attempted by Mick Jagger and David Bowie. The weird thing about Van Halen's version is that it's so disco/pop in style that one has to choke back the shock. This is a real surprise. Does it work? Not entirely.

'Little Guitars' has an acoustic feel in the intro, courtesy of Eddie, who takes the title almost literally. It opens up into a more laidback song than one might have expected, with Diamond Dave enjoying himself, even though he's slightly more subdued than one is used to. And then it's back to the covers …

A supremely confident performer, David Lee Roth (above) played a key role in establishing Van Halen as a great live act. But his personality would soon put him on collision course with Eddie.

'Big Bad Bill (Is Sweet William now)' has to go down as an odd choice. Popularised by Merle Haggard, the storyline may actually give something of a clue as to why the band (or at least some of them) thought this was appropriate. It's the story of Bill, a man feared by everyone in town as the roughest, toughest hombre of them all. Until he got hitched.

"Married life changed him somehow," croons Roth, before adding the telling line: "He's not the man they used to fear now the people call him Sweet Papa Willie Dear." Legend has it that Dave Roth chose the song, and might have had someone else in mind – dare one suggest Big Bad Ed Is Sweet Edward Now? Get the drift? Another sly dig at Eddie's marital status. Still Eddie got on manfully with the job of handling a ragtime rhythm, and there was one surprise guest on the track. Ladies and gentleman, coming out of the Orange Corner, decked in Netherlands culture, would you please welcome the Count Of The Clarinet, the Prince Of Puff … Jan Van Halen. Yep, the Van Halen brothers got their Dad down on tape.

But there was still one more surprise here. After the full tilt boogie of 'The Full Bug', Van Halen finished the album with yet another cover … 'Happy Trails'. Until then associated with the wholesome, clean-cut Roy Rogers and Dale Evans, Van Halen took this anthem to innocence and gave it a right rock twist. It has all the hallmarks of a drugfest, as the four combine in an a capella tribute to the sounds of their youth. This debauched barber-shop quartet even manage to sound slightly stoned on a track that must be strangest of their career.

And the cackles of laughter at the end are just hysterical. We all know where you're goin', boys, when you ride into the sunset!

'Diver Down' split Van Halen fans. Some loved the humour, others decried the reliance on covers and silly moments, but it still entered the US charts at Number Three. Besides, the band managed to shock the still virginal MTV network with a video for '(Oh) Pretty Woman' that featured bondage, transvestites and dwarves… not exactly the usual fare for the station. And the band called their subsequent tour 'Hide Your Sheep', a reference to the fact that Van Halen had the reputation for sexually molesting anything that moved … or, for the matter, was tethered.

> WHAT HAD HAPPENED TO VAN HALEN SO FAR WAS MERE PREPARATION FOR AN ASSAULT ON THE CHARTS AND VENUES OF THE WORLD

But the band were about the reach a crossroads. Little did they know that they were about to make the most successful album in their history, but in doing so lose one of the defining, enduring ships in their flotilla. What had happened so far was mere preparation for an assault on the charts and the roads of the world that would stun, shock and eventually shake all and sundry. We are about to enter the 1984 show – where all bets are off.

TOP OF THE PILE

It's May 1983. And Van Halen are about to play the biggest gig of their career – in fact, one of the biggest gigs of all time. The occasion is a three-day event called the US Festival, held at Glen Helen Park in San Bernardino, California.

The event had first happened in 1982, when a disparate collection of artists was brought together under the US umbrella, including The Grateful Dead, The Ramones, Talking Heads, Santana, The Police and The Cars. Now, a year on, the three days were to showcase three very different styles of music. On May 28th – day one – The Clash topped a bill that also featured Men At Work, The Stray Cats, Flock Of Seagulls and The (English) Beat. On May 30th, David Bowie was the main attraction, with Stevie Nicks, Joe Walsh, Missing Persons and U2 also on the bill. But it was what happened on May 29th that really set the festival alight. This was dubbed 'Heavy Metal Day' and included some of the hottest names in the genre. Picture this: openers Quiet Riot, followed up the order by Motley Crüe, Ozzy Osbourne, Judas Priest, Triumph, The Scorpions and finally Van Halen.

The day attracted enormous crowds – some estimated that close to 750,000 turned up to worship at the altar of metal. And Van Halen inevitably stole the show, with a bravura performance said to have been 'inspired' somewhat by what appeared to be an alcohol-fuelled David Lee Roth. The band kicked off their set with 'Romeo Delight', before heading into 'Unchained', which featured a solo from Alex. An extended 'Runnin' With The Devil' followed, before 'Jaime's Crying' and 'So This Is Love' took things down to a somewhat quieter level – well, comparatively, anyway. From here it was a straight ride into 'Little Guitars' and a Michael Anthony bass solo, which in turn took Van Halen 'Dancing In The Street'. Fans were then treated to a medley of 'Somebody Get Me A Doctor', 'Girl Gone Bad' and 'I'm So Glad', before Eddie let rip with a trademark solo.

'Dance The Night Away' was next up, with 'Secrets' leading into yet another drum solo, before a very extended – too extended – 'Everybody Wants Some' and 'Ice Cream Man' provided a lull before the storm created by the excellent '(Oh) Pretty Woman'. And it's here that Eddie finally got to hog the spotlight with an extended guitar piece (to call it a solo would be to underestimate its impact and structure). For nearly 12 minutes, the man held the audience in thrall, running through his extensive box of tricks. It was a tour de force that underlined his stature as one of the all-time greats. And while much of Van Halen's performance was sloppy and almost lacklustre, this was a shining highlight. Then it was into 'Ain't Talkin' Bout Love' and 'Bottoms Up', before the band send the fans on their way with 'You Really Got Me' and 'Happy Trails'.

This set sums up Van Halen at the time – full of the spirit of rock'n'roll, but so often lacking in substance. Ultimately, what saves them time and again is the potent combination of Eddie's genius on guitar with that of the master of ceremonies, David Lee Roth, not so much a frontman as a striding advertisement for the joys of excess. Charisma clashes with artistry – but when they work together it is irresistible.

The US Festival, organised by Apple computer founder Steve Wozniak (who lost a fortune), was the zenith of a great touring era for the band, but UK and European fans were denied yet again the chance to see a band whose popularity had never waned. Why wouldn't they come over?

"If someone could show us that we're still selling records over there and people wanna see us, Van Halen will be on the next plane over," said Roth at the time. "I'm as serious as a train wreck!" But despite the obvious evidence of demand for Van Halen in Europe, they still refused to get on that plane and make the trip. That would change in 1984, but we can't get ahead of ourselves.

Once the band had come off the road, and people could once again let their sheep roam free and untethered, Van Halen turned their attention towards a new album. But now they were under a little pressure. Despite high chart placings and hit singles, Van Halen's sales base had shrunk since those early days. Their label, Warner Brothers, needed a big selling album from the band, and not only for the sake of the Halens. They needed a hit single that would drive sales of the subsequent album.

And Van Halen also had to come to terms with a new situation. Not only were they facing serious competition from young hotshots like Motley Crüe, Bon Jovi and Ratt, but music was being presented in a new way. The MTV generation had taken hold, and it was no longer possible for a band to sell records without a video, without acknowledging the necessity for image. Of course, as Van Halen had always been visually striking this wasn't a particular problem, but having made such a bad start with MTV over the banned video for '(Oh) Pretty Woman', they were now facing the uphill task of convincing the station they could provide wholesome family entertainment.

The other factor that came into play was cost. Thanks in so small measure to Michael Jackson's elaborate video for 'Thriller', most artists were driving up budgets in order to compete and stand apart from the crowd. Van Halen would meet this challenge head on, then duck it completely in ingenious fashion.

The video in question was for the single 'Jump', released to a huge barrage of acclaim at the end of 1983. It was synth-pop with guitars. It was catchy, full of hooks and had a melody you just could not forget. It was easily the most mainstream effort ever from Van Halen, and became a massive worldwide hit for them. It was based around a simple Eddie Van Halen keyboard riff, and had the sort of impact they'd never achieved before. It was as if the band wanted to prove a point. The label wanted a hit single? OK, Van Halen would give them a hit, but not in the usual band fashion – they'd do something that could have been credited to Duran Duran or their ilk. And then they'd hope everyone would leave them alone to get back to basics on the album, which hijacked the cunning title of *1984*, and was definitely redolent of the time.

The video for 'Jump' was so simple it smacked of genius. While everybody else was trying to spend fortunes – the sort of amounts that could finance a small principality for several months – Van Halen went the other way. Using one camera and no effects, they

Guitarist and frontman, charisma clashing with artistry – but working together they are irresistible.

spent what was said to be just $500 on the shoot. It was straightforward, featured just the band, and made a massive impact. The idea was the brainchild of Roth and his new partner in crime, Pete Angelus. The pair would work increasingly closely on both Van Halen videos and the singer's subsequent solo career.

Having once again set the standards that others would have to try and follow, Van Halen then set about making sure the album was rigged for maximum impact. But while '1984' was to be a very big seller for the band, it is a very strange record. Much of it is made from bits and pieces left over from previous efforts. Indeed, 'House Of Pain' is a song the band had first worked up for their debut, and never used. What on earth was going on? Here was a record with nine songs and lasting for a shade over 32 minutes. But it was the sheer quality that bowled people over.

The album opened with a short keyboard instrumental that was, in fact, the title track. Played by Eddie Van Halen, it's more of an ambient piece that barely brought to mind Van Halen or indeed rock music at all. It was never intended as anything other than a gentle way of easing people into the record. It also hints at the glories of 'Jump' which followed immediately afterwards. The lyrics to 'Jump', says Roth, were inspired by the singer watching a crisis on TV, as a person stands on the ledge of a tall building threatening to hurl himself off. Whether this is the actuality remains a little open to question, because Roth does tend to embellish when it catches the imagination. Interestingly, in 2001, there was an incident in Omaha, Nebraska, when a man accused of domestic violence ended up on the ledge of a high building, threatening to jump. It was claimed at the time that the radio in one of the police cars gathered at the scene inadvertently blared out 'Jump'. Again, take this with a pinch of salt.

THE ALBUM WAS SHORT, BUT ITS QUALITY BOWLED EVERYONE OVER

From 'Jump', the album leaps into the joyous 'Panama', a track built around a scat from Eddie on guitar. This was Van Halen in their pomp, almost inventing everything as they went. The song has that upbeat, road hog feel of a band in complete control, and as such prepared to let the music take flight. Built on Eddie's coruscating riffs and Dave's ability to yelp, yowl and generally make his voice into an instrument, this is arguably the best song here, and contains a wonderfully fluid solo from Eddie that acts as a bridge between two distinct parts of the song yet also takes it off the usual path. Again the video is remarkable in its simplicity. It captures the Van Halen ethos and philosophy, blending live footage with some off-the-wall conceptual stuff that focuses on Dave Roth more than the others. Well, he was in charge.

'Top Jimmy' is next into the fray: a more obvious Van Halen song, albeit somewhat understated. For this reason people often overlook it when it comes to analysing the strengths of '1984'. The same can be said for 'Drop Dead Legs', which has a slow-burning groove that not surprisingly relies on Eddie's ability to vary tempo, pace and ignition. In a way, it's a very clever ploy by the Halens to drop these two songs in here between 'Panama' and 'Hot For Teacher', because it allows the listener to settle back just a bit and get used to an album full of diversity and trickery.

'Hot For Teacher' is one of those fun pieces of smut. We all know what Dave Roth is on about when he talks about "lead in his pencil". And, once again, his ability to give even the most innocent of phrases a nudge-nudge edge is very much to the fore. The song itself starts with a rush of blood from Eddie that's as fast and fluent as anything by one of the new young breed of guitar heroes – he could still turn it on if he chose. And then it's straight into a song that's a 12-bar groove – and we're talking 12 bars that serve up all manner of illicit concoctions. The band really sound like they're having the best party of all time – and the video reflected this, going for a gaudy, highly colourful approach, with everything brighter then everything else. It was a complete departure from the more monochromatic images of 'Jump' and 'Panama'.

'I'll Wait' takes us back to the synth-soaked style of 'Jump' – it's close to being a ballad with a laid-back, soporific attitude. One can almost feel the band straining to open up the song, but for once discipline is maintained. 'Girl Gone Bad' and 'House Of Pain' provide a slightly subdued finale, but they work because of the way the band managed to balance light and shade on this record.

The cover also added to the lustre – a fallen, baby-faced angel smoking and generally giving the impression of being a rock'n'roll kid, finding his own piece of heaven in the fleshpots of Mother Earth.

The album rapidly surged towards the top of the charts across the globe, putting Van Halen back on top of the hard rock pile, but things were about to get very shaky.

FORGETTING ABOUT VEGAS

Welcome to 1984. The Thought Police are everywhere, but rock'n'roll is still the alternative lifestyle for those who wish to escape the rats as they race, chasing their own tails. And nobody represents the rock dream better than Van Halen, a band who burnt the candle at both ends and took a blowtorch to the centre.

As they started out on the fateful world tour, something wasn't right in the Van Halen camp. David Lee Roth had spent years telling the rest of the crew how it should be done and where it should be done. But now his time was nearly up. The three musicians in the band – Eddie Van Halen, Alex Van Halen and Michael Anthony – were clearly fed up with Dave's antics. Things were getting so bad that to fans who saw the band on the road it appeared very much the David Lee Roth extravaganza, with the others taking a back seat and clearly not enjoying the rewards of being among the hottest bands on the planet. The *1984* album had been a critical and commercial success. But where was the spark on the road?

On assignment for *Kerrang!* Magazine, I went backstage after the Van Halen show in

Vancouver. It was an interesting sight. Diamond Dave was holding court, blasting out tunes through a hastily erected speaker system. He was having the time of his life, entertaining the gathered throng as if it was an extension of the stage set. Women were ushered in and then out again, once they'd had the allotted several seconds with the great man. But what of the rest of the band? Eddie was slumped in a corner looking like a vegetarian who'd just won the lottery and learned his prize would be paid in meat. You would never have guessed his band had just sold out yet another arena on a world tour that was the hottest ticket in every town.

The other two were nowhere to be seen. They were hiding somewhere in the bowels of the enormous venue, refusing to mingle with the backstage masses. There was a strong contrast between the atmosphere backstage and the onstage performance. That had been dominated by Dave Roth, in quite magnificent form as he pirouetted, danced, joked and wisecracked, while the band acted as if they'd rather have been anywhere else. It was almost a Diamond Dave solo show, two years before he did his first official solo tour. There was indeed trouble in paradise, and the clock was ticking.

One interesting thing was that the band now made a concerted effort to tour outside of

America, even coming to Europe. And the excitement at the band's appearance at the Castle Donington Monsters Of Rock Festival on August 18th, 1984 was palpable. They joined a bill that reflected the very best rock and metal had to offer at the time. Headlining were AC/DC, with Van Halen second on the bill, while Ozzy Osbourne, Gary Moore, Y&T, Accept and Motley Crüe completed the best line-up of talent ever assembled at the festival, which began in 1980.

> Sammy Hagar (right) seemed born to the task of fronting Van Halen. He had the pedigree, attitude and confidence he needed.

Van Halen's presentation that day was aimed solely at upstaging the headliners. David Lee Roth ensured he was outside his portable dressing room with a huge ghetto-blaster limbering up very loudly and colourfully while AC/DC were doing a photo call. The ruse worked, with most photographers excitedly distracted by the sight of this Hollywood tinsel mogul going through his warm-up exercise, shades strategically in place.

Onstage, though, Van Halen were to be something of a disappointment. While it is unarguable that so many fans had come to see them in the flesh for the first time in four years, they were lacklustre, seemingly worn down by the rigours and diversions of touring. Eddie scarcely seemed to get out of second gear, often looking as if he was by now bored with the whole game of rock'n'roll. Alex and Michael played well enough, but were a pale shadow of the behemoth rhythm section who had spent so many years rocking the globe like few others.

Diamond Dave himself seemed in good spirits, but even his usual quips didn't carry the barbed implications and sharp irony of the past. They still did enough as a band to convince the crowd to go wild in appreciation, but here was a golden opportunity lost. Of course, little did we know that this would be the last time this incarnation of Van Halen would step onto a British stage.

Following the *1984* tour Van Halen took a break, but not their frontman. Hyper as always, Roth decided to do a solo EP called *Crazy From The Heat*. Why?

"I think this is a classy move. And most of that comes from the homework. I spent a month putting this together, though it only took four or five days to actually record. I didn't write the songs. I like to construct songs, but if I don't, I don't miss it. By virtue of my own pipes, whatever I sing is going to sound like David, for good or bad. It's doesn't matter. I'm rocking. That's all I ever really wanted to do."

But while the world at large saw this EP as no more than a pleasant diversion, it was time for the crunch as far as the band were concerned. Having spent the last tour wishing they were anywhere but close to their singer, the other three seized their chance. Realising that Dave was starting to think in terms of a solo career – a desire fuelled by hit singles from *Crazy From The Heat*, with covers of the Beach Boys' 'California Girls' and Louis Prima's 'Just A Gigolo/I Ain't Got Nobody' – the band apparently made it plain that he had to either fully commit to Van Halen's next album, or …

Roth chose the latter, believing that his force of personality, financial acumen and reputation would easily carry him forward into a solo career that would be mutli-faceted, encompassing movies, TV and music. As everyone knows, after a blitzing start, things didn't go quite to plan. He never did make the leap into the sort of superstardom now enjoyed by, say, Jon Bon Jovi.

Van Halen, meantime, were left searching for a new frontman. The list of rumours was high and wide. Everyone from Motley Crue's Vince Neil to Quiet Riot's Kevin Dubrow was linked to the job. But the Halens were determined that the new man wouldn't be another giant personality like the man who'd just left. They wanted a singer with whom they could relate on a personal level, someone experienced enough to deal with being part of one of the biggest bands in the world, who would contribute musically and not go off on a wild ego trip from which there would be no return.

That meant there were few candidates. Add in that the lucky person would have to be male and American, and the list of potential new 'boys' came down to a very small number. The man Van Halen settled for was none other than Sammy Hagar, who had been with Montrose in the early 1970s, and had been following a successful solo career ever since. He had the pedigree, the attitude and the confidence to do the job. And once his name came into focus, there seemed nobody else who fitted the bill. It was as if Hagar was born to the task.

Sammy Hagar had made his reputation fronting Montrose for two albums, the classic self-titled debut and its follow-up, *Paper Money*. Montrose, led by guitarist Ronnie Montrose, should have achieved much that Van Halen went on to gain. They had the songs, the charisma, the musicianship. But, as Hagar himself pointed out earlier, the label just weren't set up to make things happen for them. So, the mistakes made on Montrose benefited Van Halen, and in 1985 they gave Hagar a job.

Reactions to the announcement of a new man in the line-up were mixed. Many David Lee Roth fans were outraged that they'd even consider carrying on without the frontman. Some felt it was an interesting and challenging choice, and looked forward to seeing what Hagar made of the band, and vice versa. There were also those – Eddie fans, really – who were delighted to see the back of Roth, and believed Van Halen would have a renewed spirit as a result. The band themselves certainly talked up the choice, seemingly relieved that the baggage carried around by their former bandmate had finally been jettisoned. After years seemingly in the musical doldrums, they could get back to making quality music and forgetting about Vegas and the like.

Hagar himself started life in the band by having what most people thought was a very silly haircut, which made him look like a reject from A Flock Of Seagulls. New career, fresh haircut. He unveiled this look at the Day On Green Festival in San Francisco, just before his confirmation in the new Van Halen line-up. But word was already out on the streets, and the man himself proved to be revealingly evasive about the whole affair when questioned on the day. Knowing that the official announcement was just days away, he contented himself with a mysterious "That's the rumour, isn't it?" followed by a knowing smirk.

Hagar not only brought more musicianship and credibility with him than would have been the case if the band had gone for one of the many David Lee Roth clones on the circuit, he was also a personality in his own right. While no motormouth in the unique style of his predecessor, he could nonetheless hold his own in interview situations, and was rarely outflanked. He'd also had one or two spats with Diamond Dave, after Roth remarked that Hagar seemed to write a lot of songs about cars, going on to speculate as to what his wife might look like.

It was all good-natured banter, and now Hagar was ready to settle into his new role – trying to fill the impossibly large shoes of the ultimate showman, Diamond David Lee Roth.

REJUVENATED

The battle for the hearts, minds and wallets of Van Halen fans happened in 1986. Former frontman David Lee Roth was first out of the blocks with his debut solo album, *Eat 'Em And Smile*. Determined to make an immediate impact, he put together what can only be described as a band that was 'Van Halen plus'. His guitarist was Steve Vai, one of many who emerged in the early part of the decade to challenge Eddie Van Halen's pre-eminence. But Vai had persisted and, thanks to the patronage of Frank Zappa and John Lydon among others, was now regarded as the hottest property around. Bassist Billy Sheehan was an in-demand session star, while drummer Greg Bissonette had all the chops, rallies and power to act as the engine room of the band.

Armed with an album full of purpose and posture, plus a striking video for the first single, 'Yankee Rose', Roth threw down the gauntlet to his former bandmates. He had the media, the momentum and the lifeforce. Surely Van Halen couldn't hope to match what he'd done? But it was a case of the tortoise and the hare. The Halens took their time in the studio, parted with longtime producer Ted Templeman (who'd thrown in his lot with Roth) and came out with a more streamlined, highly commercial album in *5150*. (The title was taken from a police radio code used when detaining a mentally disturbed person. It was also the name of Eddie's home studio, where the album was recorded.)

Producing the record were Donn Landee (who had been Templeman's sidekick for a while and so was familiar with the Van Halen methodology and mentality) and Foreigner's Mick Jones. What they delivered was a surprise – here was a band reborn. Without the quirky, often surreal approach of Roth, the gameshow zaniness of the past was dropped straight down the chute. In its place came a more disciplined, modern sound that fitted neatly into what was happening in the world of rock and metal at the time. Unpredictability was ditched, and in came a healthy respect for melody and power. New man Sammy Hagar sounded as if he'd part of the union for years, such was the manner in which he crafted the songs and fitted straight into the style.

Unmistakably Van Halen, *5150* saw the band emerge from the cul-de-sac which had been threatening them for a few years. David Lee Roth had taken the band on wild and wacky musical journeys through a whole range of styles, but what they'd lacked for years was a sense of being anchored to their musical roots. Now, with Hagar taking over, that was achieved.

Just how different the new-look Halens were was obvious with the release of the first single, 'Why Can't This Be Love?' It had a distinct synth underlay, and a tunefulness that retained integrity throughout. Almost understated, it didn't sound as if the protagonists were getting bored after 90 seconds, as had so often been the case in the Roth era. The combination of Hagar's voice – it must be admitted by even the most diehard Roth fans that

Hagar was and still is the better singer – and Eddie's rejuvenated guitar playing made this an instant hit. Inevitably, it was a chart sensation, setting the tone for what was to follow. If anything, the change had given Van Halen a boost.

The album itself didn't disappoint. There were no covers here, no rehashes of old material and no air of desperation packaged as inspiration. *5150* was a collection of highly polished, finely crafted tunes. Encouraged by Mick Jones – himself an accomplished guitarist – Eddie took up the reins and led the band's sound from the front. He was now also playing alongside a singer who was himself no mean talent on the guitar. All of which may explain why *5150* saw arguably Eddie's finest playing in the studio for years. It was calm and erudite, yet also had the power and state-of-the-art quality to make *5150* a triumph.

The band displayed a sprightly ability to make transitions from the frenzied, fret-driven 'Get Up' to the more commercially minded 'Dreams', which was to be a hit single in its own right. This line-up could also rock up a storm, as on 'Summer Nights' and 'Best Of Both Worlds', while 'Love Walks In' was the sort of power ballad that the band could never have served up in the Roth era, because it was too direct and eschewed any thought of taking a turn around irony central.

In many ways, this was a sophisticated, contemporary pop-rock record, the sort that fits neatly on any coffee table. It held no threat or implied depravity. Van Halen had grown up, and with a new production team in place they sounded alive and lively. In particular, Alex Van Halen's drum sound seemed to have been smoothed out, leaving behind the difficult patterns that were often his hallmark in the earlier days. But it was the new combination of Eddie's guitar and Sammy's voice that made the difference. The pair sounded like a match made in heaven that had spent years looking for a connection. And that may well have been the case. Hagar had worked with the egotistical, self-driven Ronnie Montrose in those far off Montrose days, while Eddie had also had problems with David Lee Roth, a man who seemed increasingly at odds with the avowed musical intentions of the guitarist. Now, each had found the ideal partner for his talents and dreams. They were revelling in the freedom achieved by combining forces.

5150 went double platinum in America within two months of its March release, topping two million sales. A little later it topped the three million mark. It appealed not only to Van Halen fans who'd followed the band for years, but also to a new audience who saw the album as representing something altogether more acceptable and radio-friendly. But Roth fans dismissed it as wallpaper music, bereft of the atmosphere and good-time affectations that had helped make the band's name in the first place. So how did *5150* stack up against *Eat 'Em And Smile*? In fact, not at all. Here were two radically different beasts. Roth was developing the sound of classic Van Halen, going for a line-up and approach that he felt would prove who had been the life and soul of the Halen party. He succeeded, with Steve Vai in particular giving vent to some astonishing musical moments on guitar. Van Halen, meanwhile, had no interest in the past. They were going into differing areas. Perhaps not as challenging and experimental as they had been (although the overlapping bar conversations at the end of 'Inside' certainly brought a surreal element into play), the band didn't really care too much about what had gone before. People had

> Working with a sympathetic vocalist at last, Eddie now revelled in a live show that brought music to the fore.

already made choices – Pete Angelus and Ted Templeman went with Roth – and those who remained were made aware that times had changed. This was a band moving forward, determined to head towards middle age by taking on different influences and attitudes.

The subsequent tour was also well received. Van Halen combined the old and new material well in the set, and people quickly got used to the fact that here was an approach that was diametrically opposed to what had gone before. Hagar would even occasionally strap on a guitar and join the fray. Eddie's role had also altered. He was far more to the fore than had been the case in the recent past. He seemed more confident in a stage set that augmented the music rather than overshadowing it. This time it was about the songs and the musicians, not the antics of the frontman, however important he had been in making Van Halen great in the first place.

So, Van Halen had won their first battle – they'd shown a clean pair of heels to Dave Roth. They were outselling him on both the record and live fronts. They had successfully re-invented themselves, while he was living gloriously in the past. The new Van Halen may have lacked the easy charm and charisma of what had gone before, but it was a trade-off. Too many years seemingly in thrall to Diamond Dave – even if he was one of the all-time greats – may have taken their toll towards the end of their relationship, but that was all forgotten. For Van Halen circa 1986 everything pointed to a bright future. And as the next years unfurled, Roth's influence would definitely wane, while his one-time friends and colleagues would maintain a consistency that surprised.

STARTING TO CREAK

If *5150* proved that Van Halen's hold on their commercial market was as strong as ever, it also displayed a curious change in their strategy. No longer interested in the 'rock'n'roll music with attitude' approach that littered their glory days with Dave Lee Roth, the band seemed content to grow up – and do it with a certain grace. Moreover, given the fact that they had little love for their former singer (mutual antipathy would be more accurate at this time), there may have been a certain satisfaction (albeit in private) as the shine came off the Diamond. He may have started out as a solo artist with a flourish, panache and a high profile, but by the time 1988 rolled around, he was already in decline, as *Skyscraper* (the follow-up to *Eat 'Em And Smile*) brought a sales dip – one that he has never been able to arrest. What's more, he seemed to be on a self-destructive course, proving that he wasn't a true band leader, as the strongest possible band line-up started to come apart.

Van Halen, for their part, were closer-knit than ever. Hagar had settled in well, and the whole band felt the sales of *5150* augured well for the future. What a shame, then, that they rapidly went into a steep decline, at least artistically. Why? Maybe it was an inability to develop a style and stick with it. While Hagar had helped to bring out a different side to the music – one that saw Van Halen embrace the pop-rock market like never before – they quickly became content with their lot, locking the door on any chance of developing their talents further.

For Eddie Van Halen, this must have been particularly galling. Having spent years fighting a vain battle against the Roth-fuelled excesses, now he had to fight against middle-aged contentment. Hagar, for his part, seemed to accept what was being offered. His coffers were swelling, and he no longer had to fight as hard to make an impact. Why is it that a band as good as Van Halen could never get themselves into the frame of mind to make a lasting and evolving impact? Maybe it's simply because the talent involved was so extreme and uncontrollable. It was, and remains, frustrating that a band with so much to offer could continually sell themselves short.

OU812 was released in 1988, with the band taking control of the production – a

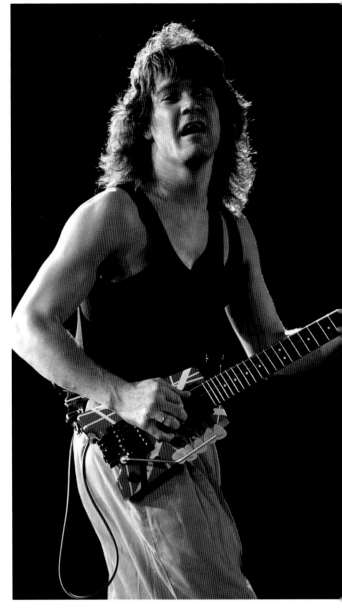

good example of how they sold themselves short. While Mick Jones had brought an extra dimension to *5150* and allowed the music to breathe and grow, this time around things got just a shade distorted and derailed. The opening track, 'Mine All Mine', is typical of the problem. A strong song, it is swamped in synthesizers, which seem to overshadow Eddie Van Halen's guitar: he seems happier here to play keyboards and dabble with their sound structures rather than going for the throat on guitar, which was still his forte. Eddie needed someone outside of the band to stand back, and give a more objective, dispassionate view on sound and instrument balance.

'When It's Love' is yet another richly tapestried pop-rock anthem. But while 'Why Can't This Be Love' – or even 'Jump' – made the listener feel part of the song, simply because of a irresistible edge, this one lacks real heart and commitment. It is so bathed in synth that even Sammy Hagar – a man who can be relied upon to make even a takeaway menu seem lyrically convincing – is a little lost and distant from it all.

'A.F.U. (Naturally Wired)' is more of an in-your-face rocker, the sort that Van Halen could do so well when the mood took them. Hagar's voice seems almost relieved to be able to get to grips with something a little more stirring, as the blood finally pumps. But Eddie's guitar tones are once again at odds with what's required. For a man who had virtually re-invented the electric guitar a decade previously, he now seemed as if he'd fallen out of love with the instrument.

'Cabo Wabo', which was to become the name of Hagar's restaurant in Mexico, is one of the worst pieces of self-indulgence Van Halen had ever cooked up. It's laborious, at times painfully so, and lacks the punch and panache that had stood Van Halen in good stead for so long. Fortunately, 'Source Of Infection' is a lot more in the groove, pounding out the rhythms, as Eddie finally gets to grips with the demands of a song that needs a driving guitar. This time it gets what's needed, as the master swoops and swirls while keeping very much to the script.

But having got into a more rocking mode, the band then revert to synth-pop for 'Feels So Good', which certainly does not. It's tired, listless and lacks any energetic guitar feel. One must wonder what on earth was going through their collective heads as they plumbed the depths of the worst type of 1980s pop.

'Finish What Ya Started' is a song lost in its own creation. Put simply, it's dull, dull, dull. Van Halen seemed to be trying to recreate the glories of the Roth era, maybe trying to prove that they could this sort of thing without Dave. They couldn't. Eddie's jingly-jangly guitar style might have worked up against a scat sultan like Dave Roth, but Hagar's more disciplined approach does the song no favours. A huge mistake. 'Black And Blue' is another bad error, a musical mess accentuated by some of the crassest lyrics in the band's history. When Hagar yelps,

> SOME FANS WERE ASKING: HOW MUCH LIFE IS LEFT IN THIS MONSTER?

"Bitch sure got the rhythm, the harder the better, the wetter the better … yo mama", it leaves the listener cringing at the teenage ineptitude of it all.

'Sucker In A 3 Piece' barely lifts the mood, as once again the band get lost in a party atmosphere. The song cries out for the Roth touch, and for a producer to give it direction. It's the ultimate song for a party where nobody turns up. Finally, there's a misguided cover of 'A Apolitical Blues' by the late Lowell George. Unlike many of the covers the band attempted in the Dave Roth era, this is pointless drivel, offering nothing but a space filler.

OU812 sold well, very well, maintaining the illusion that everything in the Van Halen camp was running on well-oiled tracks. In fact, the band were already starting to creak. Ideas were at a premium, and while crowds flocked to see them live, the question some were starting to ask was how much life was left in this monster?

BATTERED AND BRUISED

Van Halen — or Van Hagar as some still prefer to call them — were very much
on top of their game as the 1980s sighed for one last time, giving way to the 1990s and the
birth of grunge. But, while they gathered their forces, marshalled resources and prepared to
follow up *OU812*, the band took a disastrous turn with possibly the worst album of their
career to date, the appallingly trite *For Unlawful Carnal Knowledge*. Even the title was lame.

Having learnt their lesson on *OU812*, the band decided to bring in veteran Andy Johns
and old pal Ted Templeman on the production side. The trouble was that, while Van Halen
went for a more direct, rockier sound this time around, the material was generally poor,
certainly well below the standards they had set themselves with *5150* five years previously.

What went wrong? In all honesty, the band's creative juices had started to dry up when
OU812 went into production. The initial burst of clarity and focus that suffused the first
album with Hagar hadn't lasted too long. And Eddie, in particular, seemed to lose a lot of
momentum. His guitar playing was suffering from a lack of heart and passion. He no longer
seemed able to raise his game to take on the challenges of a new generation of guitar heroes,
many of whom had been inspired by his performances way back in the early days of Van
Halen.

One also wonders whether the friction between David Lee Roth and Eddie Van Halen had
been principally responsible for some of the guitarist's most inspired moments. He was the
man who gave the electric guitar a new twist just when it seemed we'd heard it all before.
Now, here he was, seemingly out of ideas and in desperate need of a shot of inspiration from
somewhere — anywhere. He wasn't to get it on *For Unlawful Carnal Knowledge*.

And yet the album does start off promisingly. Opening shot 'Poundcake' has a heavy
groove, with a decent riff from the master blaster on guitar, and even incorporates the sound
of a drill. The rhythm section is almost nasty and twisted, while Hagar lays down the vocal
law in a fashion that actually brings to mind his solo days. This was a rousing, impressive
start that, unfortunately, the band were not able to capitalize on. The rest of the album simply
sounded like they were disinterested and virtually running on empty.

'Spanked' is of interest, because Eddie carts in a six-string bass and tries something a
little different, but it doesn't really come off, although he does produce a neatly packaged,
more conventional guitar motif right at the climax. So much more might have been possible
with that bass, given Eddie's dexterity, but the band were seemingly reverting back to that
old philosophy of minimum effort.

'Right Now' gets close to the anthemic, even possessing a distinctly hummable chorus,
with Eddie once again hinting at the awesome power and presence he was always capable of
generating. But this is a rarity on an album that topples over as it looks for a direction. 'Top
Of The World' is typical of where things were falling apart. The band seem to be trying to

cruise into a slick hard rock lane, with Hagar clearly forcing the pace, but something holds them back – and that something is their lack of commitment to what's being hammered out. There are points on *For Unlawful Carnal Knowledge* when Van Halen sound so bored and fed up, the wonder is that they got to complete the record at all. Maybe the hint is in the song 'The Dream Is Over', with the suggestion that, after so many years pounding the road and the studio, the band were battered and bruised. They needed a break – desperately.

But there was none coming. Van Halen were soon back out on tour, promoting an album they didn't seem to believe in, and trying to decide whether it was all worth the bother. Worse still, there were the first signs of a rift between the three founders and Hagar. Not a massive one, but enough to start rumours that perhaps all wasn't well in paradise.

However, the band bought themselves some valuable time with the release of the disjointed double live CD *Live: Right here, Right Now* in 1993. Amazingly, despite a whole history of great shows over the years, Van Halen had never done a live album before. This should surely have been done in the Dave Roth era, when they were on top of their form and delivering performances that set the world on fire. But, better late than never, the band finally got around to selecting songs for what was something of a retrospective live record.

Certain performances dated back to 1985, when Hagar first joined the band. But over all there's far too much emphasis on the *For Unlawful Carnal Knowledge* material; amazingly, ten tracks are taken from this release. And only a handful of Roth era songs are given an airing. It is salutary to reflect on how Hagar handles the older songs. While he is a better singer than his predecessor, he certainly cannot do justice to 'Ain't Talkin' 'Bout Love', 'Jump', 'Panama' or 'You Really Got Me'. As with the Ozzy versus Dio debate in the Black Sabbath camp, there's no question that the humour, charm, charisma and personality of the original Van Halen frontman imbued those songs with life, something nobody else could match. Sure, Roth could never have done justice to something like 'Why Can't This be Love?', but would he actually have wanted to?

Inevitably, *Live: Right Here, Right Now* is a patchwork at best, and really seems to have been designed to buy the band valuable time while they sorted out where to go next. However, the true star of the show is Eddie Van Halen. His playing throughout is of the highest quality, and his solos touch heights he had rarely reached in the studio over the years. It was as if the whole record had been carefully put together as a tribute to a man who was the most important rock guitarist to emerge since the death of Jimi Hendrix. Listening to some of his work here reveals the talent and sublime touch of the man.

While all this was going on, David Lee Roth was trying to salvage a career that was in steep decline. There were even rumours at this time that he might consider rejoining Van Halen should Sammy Hagar leave. Roth's problem was that, while he was a stunning, unique frontman, he couldn't lead a band. The line-up he'd so carefully put together at the start of his solo career had now fallen apart, and those who'd been brought in as replacements were not of the same high standard. In a different way, he was facing a crisis.

For Van Halen, the mid-1990s were about to become a period of turbulence and change. But first, at least, they got back on track with an album that was more focused and directed than anything they'd done since *5150*. 1995's *Balance* was to prove there was life left in these old dogs – and it was also the signal for another singer change.

SENSATIONAL CIRCUMSTANCES

In 1995, Van Halen seemed to find their feet once more with the aptly titled *Balance*. In many respects, this is the album that saw Eddie Van Halen exert most control, varying the pace and trying to find a way forward for the band. With the indefatigable Bruce Fairbairn as producer and ally, the guitarist mixes it up more than he had done for ages, and Sammy Hagar is a willing collaborator. The problem is with Michael Anthony and Alex Van Halen, who are percussive, metronomic and steady, but never seem to get in the mood. When Eddie calls for subtlety or a swift change of velocity, he gets nothing from his longtime partners. They're locked in a groove loop, seemingly unable to change the pattern.

Fairbairn, though, concentrates his efforts on the guitarist, who seems to have been given a fresh lease of life by a producer who encourages him to take risks and explore new avenues. This isn't the tired, outdated and uninterested man of recent albums. Here is a musician letting fly.

Eddie Van Halen discussed *Balance* with Smashing Pumpkins' mainman Billy Corgan during an interview the latter conducted with him for *Guitar World* magazine:

"*For Unlawful Carnal Knowledge* took a year to record; that's why the playing on it might sound somewhat laboured. *Balance*, on the other hand, was written and recorded in only four months, so the whole process was more immediate. I also think our producer, Bruce Fairbairn, had something to do with the sense of excitement on *Balance*. Instead of arguing with me, he encouraged me to pursue my own ideas. He was somebody I could relate to. Together we were able to create a vibe."

The opening song, 'The Seventh Seal', sets the tone with a strong, earthy vibe that's appropriately apocalyptic in vision and momentum. Eddie's playing hits top form very quickly and retains its style and posture throughout. This song was to get Van Halen a Grammy nomination. They also picked up an American Music Awards nomination for their work on *Balance*. That was at the start of 1996; four years earlier they had won a Grammy in the 'Best Hard Rock Performance With Vocals' category as recognition for the album *For Unlawful Carnal Knowledge*.

Among the other highlights on an album littered with good moments are 'Don't Tell Me (What Love Can Do)', which deals with the problems of growing up in the turbulent world of the last decade of the nearly dead century, and 'Amsterdam', which is something of a good-time number, extolling the virtues of the capital city in question.

The record itself was warmly received, and again sold well, fuelled principally by the success of 'Don't Tell Me…' There was a genuine feeling that Van Halen were back on the pace and moving forward. Everything seemed positive in the garden, as the *Balance* tour

whipped them around the globe. But it was all about to fall apart, with Hagar parting from Van Halen in sensational circumstances. Rumours had been rife for months that Hagar was out of the band, that he'd either been fired or quit, depending on whose side you took. In June 1996, the official announcement came from SRO, the band's management: Hagar out… Diamond Dave back in! At least, Roth was returning to record two new songs for a 'Best Of' collection.

As for Hagar, what did happen? Eddie Van Halen put it down to new-found sobriety opening his eyes to Sammy's deficiencies as a lyricist. The guitarist had spent years vainly battling against drink and drugs addiction, seemingly an insurmountable problem. But then in 1994 (October 2nd, to be precise), he finally quit.

"I've slipped a few times," he said in 1998 to *Metal Hammer* magazine. "I'll have a glass of wine every now and then, but I have not been drunk. I'll have a glass of wine, but I might not even finish it. I think that half the reason why I was that way was because I was so beat down to the point of, 'Keep Eddie drunk and get the best of him.' It ain't like that no more. I don't even know if I'm an alcoholic or not. I sure don't crave it, I really don't."

The turning point for Eddie in his attempts to give up these addictions came one night when he staggered home, and found his son, Wolfgang, staring at him:

"I stumbled in around 8:30 in the morning. I walked in the door and he stood there and looked at me: 'Daddy, what's the matter?' I mean, he could tell something was wrong by just looking at me. I didn't say anything, I just tripped and fell. This is really hard for me to talk about. [Eddie's eyes turn glossy and tears start forming.] If it hadn't been for that ... You know, kids are so pure and you can't fool them. You can't pull any shit on them."

When he came out of his long haze, Eddie suddenly started to look seriously at the lyrics written by Hagar, and was less than impressed.

> HAGAR SPENT YEARS BITTER AND ANGRY ABOUT THE WAY HE WAS TREATED BY THE BAND – BUT IT WASN'T TO BE THE END

"I listened to the songs and I like the music, but I can't believe that I let some of the lyrics go. I did my thing, but it's not something I condone or tried to push. Sammy would be on stage half shitfaced toasting to my sobriety! If that ain't a fucking crazy situation I don't know what is. That's beyond strange."

The result was a major falling-out between the two friends, and the subsequent firing of the singer, on Father's Day. Hagar was to spend years very bitter and angry at the way he was treated by the band, although in typical Van Halen style, this wasn't to be the end of his relationship with them.

"It actually made it easier for me when they got David Lee Roth back in the band for me to go, 'Well, the hell with you guys!'" Hagar told *Undercover News* in 1999. "This is like really back-stabbing. They were rehearsing with Roth for two weeks before I even found out about it. After ten great years of camaraderie they turn on me like that."

Eddie Van Halen explained to *Guitar World* magazine how Roth came to be back in the picture...

"He happened to call me around the same time Sammy quit, because Warner Bros had notified him that *Greatest Hits* was going to come out, and he had a few questions about the packaging and other details. I told him I didn't know yet, but would let him know next week. We were on the phone for about 45 minutes and we apologized for things we had said back in high school - even junior high. It was probably one of the best conversations I've ever had with him. Especially since as long as I've known him, we were never really friends. We were just from different planets. But band-wise, it just seemed to work. A few days later, instead of calling him, I decided to drive over to his house and fill him in."

Roth's return was being treated with caution by all concerned. He came back officially just to record two new tracks for *The Best Of Van Halen Volume One*, namely 'Me Wise Magic' and 'Can't Get This Stuff No More'. Neither is especially memorable. They really hint at a band and singer tentatively feeling their way forward. In fact, it has been argued that neither party was giving 100 per cent to the project. There was a sense that this would be temporary, so why give away the best you've got?

Most fans expected this fist step to lead to an announcement of a full-blown reunion tour and album. It never happened. Things fell apart at the moment when they seemed about to be cemented. In September 1996, the whole band – including Roth – appeared together in public for the first time since their parting more than a decade previously. It was at the MTV Video Music Awards. They received an ecstatic response – a standing ovation. But Diamond Dave's expected ebullience when he grabbed the microphone didn't go down at all well with his bandmates. A major row erupted backstage between the singer and Eddie Van Halen – the reunion was off the agenda.

Subsequently, Roth claimed he was set up by the rest of the band. They allowed him to take the microphone, to give them an excuse to ditch a reformation about which they were having second thoughts. For their part, the band believed that working on the two new tracks with their one-time singer had exposed serious musical differences. They felt it couldn't work, and Diamond Dave's 'antics' at the MTV Awards compounded their reluctance, and persuaded them to ditch the plan.

So, what could the band do now? They had no singer, no re-union, only an uncertain future. At which point, they made the biggest mistake of their career.

BOGGED DOWN

The abrupt end to the expected re-union with David Lee Roth left Van Halen without a game plan for the future. But Eddie saw no other way forward.

"Everything went to pieces at the MTV Video Awards," he explained. "After we went out on stage to present an award to Beck, we started doing some interviews, and I was just telling the truth: 'If we do a tour we'll have to write and record a new record. But before any of that can happen, I have hip replacement scheduled for December 16, and that's going to put me out of commission for four to six months.'

"After doing a couple of these interviews, Dave's attitude changed. I asked him what was wrong, and he said, 'Well, what's with this hip thing? Would you stop mentioning the hip thing?' I said, 'Okay, no problem. In the next interview I won't say a word about my hip.' He turned to me and said, 'You fuckin' better not.' And man, I lost it! I yelled, 'You muthafucker, don't ever talk to me or anybody like that again. Don't bother calling me anymore.' I thought he had changed, but two minutes on stage and a half-assed standing ovation and he turned right back into the old Dave that I hated."

So who could Van Halen turn to? The answer was a surprise: former Extreme man Gary Cherone. Now, Boston band Extreme had enjoyed a decent amount of success in the late 1980s, fuelled specifically by the hit ballad 'More Than Words'. Cherone had proven himself to be a personable frontman, if a little lacking in personality. But the main star of the band was guitarist Nuno Bettencourt, regarded as one of the best of a new breed of axe heroes. It was he who gave Extreme what individuality they possessed. And by the mid-1990s they'd split up, having failed to move their career on from the chart blandness of 'More Than Words'.

In many ways, they were a diluted Van Halen, so the choice of Cherone to front the new-look Halen was seemingly logical.

But many fans were stunned at this rather drab choice. Of course, the protagonists all put up a very positive front, extolled the virtues of the latest line-up.

"Gary can sing anything," Eddie Van Halen said at the time. "He can sing hard rock and sing like an angel. He's a talent from heaven. He sings from the heart. There's no contrived anything with him."

"God threw this in my lap," added Cherone. "The new record is going to be wild. It's going to be eclectic, and will be a new birth for everybody. And Eddie is just unbelievable. He goes nonstop and can write songs at 8 am or 4am, it doesn't matter. Everybody knows what he can do with a guitar, but you should see him sit at a piano and play these beautiful classical melodies. Eddie called me out of the blue. We hit it off as people first, then hit it off musically."

Not that anyone else really felt any confidence that Van Halen would enjoy a renaissance with the new singer. The doom-mongers were proven to be correct, as the *Van Halen III* album (released in 1998) turned out to be a disaster. Both artistically and commercially it was the worst of the band's career. With Mike Post given the unenviable task of trying to make it work, the band never even get on to the starting blocks. Barely able to raise a whimper, they struggle with no sign of inspiration or perspiration. Cherone sounds so out of his depth that one must feel a little sympathy for his plight, especially as he's given no help at all by his new bandmates, with Eddie rarely capable of getting into gear.

There is a hint that the band were trying to expand their sound, but for the most part they get bogged down in clichéd arena rock; it was as if the activities and changes of the previous two years had finally taken their toll. They sound tired, with no energy or desire, a band who'd run their course and should now seriously consider retirement.

Not surprisingly, the inevitable tour was poorly attended. Nobody saw this line-up as a true representation of Van Halen's worth. And, if the band were to stop the rot, then they had to cut their losses, admit the mistake and get rid of Cherone. It was something they did at the end of 1999. Ironically, for the first time, one got the feeling that the decision to part with a singer was taken with more than a touch of disappointment. Cherone had given his all, he got on with the other three in the band on a personal level. But it didn't fire the imagination.

> Eddie Van Halen's efforts could not disguise the fact that the band had become bogged down in clichéd stadium rock.

"I had a great time singing with the band and I wish Eddie, Alex and Michael all the best," said a sad Cherone. "Who knows, I might get the chance to work with Eddie on a separate project one day. We have spoken about it."

"Gary is a brother and he and I will continue to have a personal and musical relationship," added Eddie, backing up the feeling that there was mutual respect.

So, what next? The first name in the frame was a real shock: Whitesnake leader David Coverdale. He was mentioned in August of that year as a possible new frontman for Van Halen. It was even being reported on the Internet – that constant source of misinformation – that Coverdale and the Van Halen brothers had recorded more than 20 songs, including three new ones, to see how the relationship might pan out. The removal of Cherone fuelled those stories, and things reached fever pitch when the singer allegedly gave an interview revealing that these recording sessions had indeed happened, and that discussions were ongoing.

Subsequently, though, the interview was shown never to have happened, and the Coverdale camp issued a statement denying such links. Interestingly, though, a spokesman for the one-time Deep Purple man did leave the door slightly ajar for a collaboration by suggesting the vocalist might prove receptive to the idea of working with Alex and Eddie Van Halen on a separate project, along similar lines to the one that brought him together with another guitar legend, Jimmy Page, in 1993. But to this day, nothing further has been said on the matter.

However, all thoughts about a future for Van Halen had to be put on indefinite hold when Eddie admitted publicly that he was about to face the most difficult battle of his life – and for his life.

DIFFICULT EVENTS

In May 2000, Van Halen officially confirmed what had been rumoured for some while: Eddie Van Halen was being treated for cancer. The statement from the band was as follows:

"The University of Texas M.D. Anderson Cancer Center confirms that guitarist Eddie Van Halen visited the Houston center yesterday (May 25) as an outpatient. According to M.D. Anderson doctors, Eddie is planning to begin an outpatient clinical trial to prevent cancer. No further information is being released at this time."

Eddie was actually suffering from cancer of the tongue, something that is thought to have been brought on as a result of the years he spent hitting the bottle. For the guitarist it was yet another phase in his ongoing health battles, firstly with addiction, then with his right hip (which has been replaced). Now, it was cancer that tried to stare him down.

"I believe that God doesn't lay this on unless you are supposed to learn something," Eddie told *Maximum Golf* magazine. "I know I'm kicking its ass out. The way I look at it is like this, I've run too many red lights and gotten away with it for a long time, but it kinda caught up with me. And boy, I've learned more in the last year and a half than I ever thought I'd learn in a lifetime. Sometimes when things are in front of your face, you don't see them. It seems simple, but all that really matters to me is my son and my wife. Everything and everybody else can pretty much kiss my ass. Even making music – which is pretty much my life – takes a back seat to my family and my health.

"I used to get wasted because I didn't know how to act. I was, and still am, very uncomfortable being a so-called 'rock star'. I would get so hammered that I would make a complete fool out of myself. I was like, 'Okay, I'm a rock star. Now what is that?' I sure as hell didn't know - regardless of whether I was drunk or straight. So I figured I might as well go straight, because drunk I was a complete idiot; straight, at least I have the chance of being just half an idiot. Funny thing is, after all these years, I still don't have a clue what a 'rock star' is."

Everyone connected with the guitarist was hoping and praying he'd pull through this latest crisis in an eventful life. And within two years, the good news had been announced: after extensive treatment, he was now declared free of cancer.

"I know I promised I'd get back to you, and I'm sorry for the delay, but I wanted to let you all know that I've just gotten a 100 per cent clean bill of health – from head to toe," he wrote on the band's website, www.van-halen.com. It was a huge relief for everyone, as the treatment he'd been undergoing proved to have done the job. Now, finally, Eddie and the band could think about whether there was to be any sort of a future for them. But first there was another scenario that Eddie had to face.

In July 2002, he and his wife Valerie revealed that they'd separated the previous October. "We're friends," said the 47-year-old guitarist. "We love each other. We're just separated. I can't tell you if it will lead to a divorce, because I don't know."

It seemed that years of standing by her husband as he battled a series of nightmares had finally proven to be too much for the famed TV actress. She had moved out of the couple's home in San Fernando Valley, and was now considering whether she really wanted to make this permanent. It was just another episode in the soap opera life that Eddie Van Halen had come to inhabit over the years.

"Well, a lot happened to me [in the last six years]," he told *Guitar World* magazine. "I had hip-replacement surgery, I beat cancer and my marriage ended. Those were all important and difficult events, and I needed time to deal with them. There was nothing really mysterious about any of it, but all three of those things were extremely personal, and I didn't feel the need to share them with the public. But I never stopped making music. I worked through them, and I discovered there was a light at the end of the tunnel – and it wasn't an oncoming train. It changed my life forever. I'm back, I'm black and I'm chasing young white meat! There is nothing that can keep me down. Whatever stands before me I will deal with."

Now, it was time to get the juggernaut called Van Halen back on track. The Van Halen brothers and Michael Anthony had to decide exactly who would sing in the revamped line-up. And for most people, the choice was obvious: it lay between Sammy Hagar and David Lee Roth. No-one else could surely come into the frame. In order to go forward, the band would now have to go back to their illustrious past.

HEAVYWEIGHT FACE-OFF

In the Summer of 2002, Sammy Hagar and David Lee Roth teamed up for a fight-to-the-finish tour of America. Attracting enormous attention, the pair billed it as some sort of travelling heavyweight face-off. In many ways, it was almost an elimination contest to see who would take their rightful place back with Van Halen.

"If Sammy Hagar and David Lee Roth can do a tour together, there could be hope for the Middle East. We could straighten them fools out," laughed Hagar at the time. "There are always fears that this will look cheap. It's not cheap. It's very cool. If Van Halen were out there playing with another singer, we wouldn't bother. But they've been hiding for so long. Dave and I are giving fans the gift they deserve, and we'll try to blow each other off the stage."

"This is a bit of Americana," added Diamond Dave. "The period I was quarterback for Van Halen is as familiar as McDonald's arches and the Nike swoosh. It was my music, too. I wrote half of every song, half the musical changes and chord patterns, every single title. I designed the show and told you to show up."

The tour was a huge financial success, but the tensions between the two former Van Halen frontmen soon reached fever pitch. While they might both have been electrifying onstage, attempting to outdo each other in a way that was all to the good for the fans, trouble was never far away.

"My show is interactive, and Dave's show is all about, 'Watch me … watch me at all times'," Hagar told *Music's Bottom Line* magazine in Cleveland. "The first night in Cleveland, he wasn't so bad, that was his best show … As that tour went on though, he deteriorated … There were nights where he was just like … Hearing his voice from the backstage, we'd be back there laughing, it was sad.

"He'd be opening for us, and he'd be driving all night on that bus smoking cigarettes, doing who knows what … and the next night he'd get to the gig and go right straight onstage and we'd be backstage … It was embarrassing, because we'd be back there just laughing at him — he sounded like a guy imitating David Lee Roth …

"I threw a party: Dave thought he WAS the party! Like, 'Watch me … I'm having a party you fuckers!' He's pissing on them, sprinkling his whiskey on them and shit … he treated the audience like shit."

It was clear from most reports that, while Dave Roth concentrated almost solely on the songs he'd helped to make famous during his sojourn with Van Halen, he was struggling to keep up with Hagar, who was spanning his entire career (pre-Van Halen and post-Van Halen, as well as Montrose and his solo stuff). There was only to be one winner on this tour, and his initials were not 'DLR'.

Roth himself, though, took a few choice swipes at his touring partner, when he spoke to *The Press Of Atlantic City* newspaper in June 2003:

"The truth is we had a great time [touring together] last year. Like I said to him on the way in, 'Let's do a retrospective of one of the greatest barbecue bands in the history of the sport. You play yours and I'll play mine. It may be the only time people will get a chance to hear all of the songs in one night.' So I played my 22 huge hits and he played his three or four. I'd have him back to open up for me tomorrow if he would do it. My self-esteem is not a question. It's not ego. I know I'm not the best writer in the history of rock. There were better ... but it's about ambition. And no one can top me in that department."

It was during the Summer of 2003 that the re-union rumours began to bubble back to the surface. Dave Roth seemed to be the early frontrunner, with reports even suggesting that he'd had meetings with his one-time bandmates, and they'd even started work on new songs. Here's what Roth said to *The Oregonian* newspaper:

"There will have to be an intervention with Eddie before we even start talking again about going out on tour or making an album. I don't want to get everybody worked up again with all of the millions of dollars of expectations. On the positive side, I think 'Hope springs eternal' is an axiom to live by."

It seemed that Roth wasn't prepared to rule himself out of the running for a re-union. As for Hagar...

"The Sammy fans out there think that the only way that Van Halen's ever going to do it is to get back with me. The Dave fans would love to see a reunion, but if they've seen Dave recently, I think that they've gotta know ... I'm not down on Dave ... Well, yes I am down on Dave, but he became an asshole on that tour. I was all for Dave for a while, when I approached him and said, 'Let's do this tour together.' I was all for Dave, but after going out there with him and seeing how he is on stage and listening to his voice ... I mean, he can't do it. He's not what he used to be, and there's no question about it.

"So even those hardcore Dave fans who think they want to see that reunion, it would be one time for the big-time, and then it would be like, 'Whoa!' They can't make a new record with Dave ... They tried that! If they could do it ... they tried with Dave three times, and they couldn't do it, so ... HE couldn't do it, it's not them, it's him. And with me, one thing of course is that at least we could do all the material! I mean, we know that I can sing ALL the material, I mean ... I think I'm a better singer now than I was when I was in the band, that's the truth."

So, what would Van Halen do? It seemed as if both Hagar and Roth were prepared to talk to the band. But by September 2003, things seemed to have cooled, at least as far as Hagar was concerned when he spoke to *Goldmine* magazine:

"There is not a Van Halen. I mean, I hate to break the news to all these people, but there is not. Michael Anthony plays with me part-time, and if it wasn't for me just being crazy about my wonderful bass player Mona, who I think is the greatest, Mike would be in my band right now. And as far as I'm concerned, if there's no Sammy, no Mike, or no David Lee Roth in Van Halen, then there's Eddie and Alex Van Halen, and that is not Van Halen. I'm sure they're capable of putting together a great band, or doing great solo projects, whatever they decide to do. But I don't think that the world is going to buy it as Van Halen without at least two or more of the original kind of members. So there really is no Van Halen."

So, that was it? Er, not quite. It was reported that Hagar had actually met up with *5150* producer Mick Jones in August 2003, and the latter had put him touch with Alex Van Halen.

This in turn, it was being suggested, had led to the pair meeting up the next month. By October 2003, Hagar and Eddie were talking. Mostly it was about rumours that Warner Brothers would start to repackage and reissue the Van Halen back catalogue without any input from the band, and the concerns all the musicians felt about this.

But the talks did touch upon Hagar's return to the line-up. Inside sources were suggesting that Hagar had persuaded the Van Halen brothers to talk to his manager, Irving Azoff, about taking on the band. And that there had also been informal chats about how any reunion would work, given the fact that Hagar wasn't keen to give up his other band, The Waboritas (with whom he'd recorded solo albums). Eddie Van Halen apparently suggested a Genesis-style relationship, with Van Halen coming together for an album and tour, leaving each member free to pursue other projects.

So, by the end of 2003, the reformation was a reality in all but an official statement, which surely couldn't be long in coming. And then, in March 2004, the worst kept secret in rock was in the public domain: Van Hagar were back.

JUST GETTING STARTED

"It was a complete love-fest. The whole point of being older is, you kind of forget what happened or whatever you said. All that stuff goes out the window. We said, 'Forget it.' Rather than go to therapy like some of these other bands, we're gonna forget, like it never happened. That's done and this is right now and we're going for it."

That's the way Sammy Hagar saw his return to Van Halen. As for what he'd said in the past, when the split had happened in 1996, Hagar had this to say to shock-jock Howard Stern:

"Things change. People wake up one morning and feel different. I was being honest back then … I have no explanation [for] anything. It's like, it's a rock'n'roll band. Let's start right there, OK? Like the Rolling Stones, or anybody else. Mick and Keith are always gonna kill each other … and then they go out and tour and do great.

"[When we met up] Ed says, 'Man, wait till you hear this stuff I've been working on; I've been jamming with Al every day.' And so I was interested. I love music. There's no question about the brilliance of the music of Van Halen from the beginning till the day they die. So, when I heard the music, it was just extremely inspiring. I started writing lyrics. We started jamming. We just jammed. That's what it was."

The band decided that they should release a new compilation album called *The Best Of*

Both Worlds, a double CD that would span their career from Roth to Hagar, and that they should include three new songs, recorded with Hagar. These are 'It's About Time', 'Up For Breakfast' and 'Learning To See'. This would also mark the end of the band's long association with the Warner Bros label, who had decided to part with the legendary rockers.

But on the road, the excitement was palpable, as Van Halen started their comeback on June 11th, 2004 in Greensboro Coliseum, North Carolina. The set list reveals that the band were very much focusing on the Hagar era as they began their first tour in six years: 'Jump', 'Runaround', 'Humans Being', 'Up For Breakfast', Michael Anthony solo, 'Somebody Get Me A Doctor', 'Poundcake', 'It's About Time', Alex Van Halen solo, 'Top Of The World', 'Unchained', 'Why Can't This Be Love?', 'Eagles Fly', 'Deeper Kind Of Love', 'Learning To See', 'Best Of Both Worlds', Eddie Van Halen solo, 'Dreams', 'Ain't Talkin' 'Bout Love', 'Right Now', 'You Really Got Me', 'Panama', 'When It's Love'.

The tour lasted until late 2004. Any future plans remain on hold. Rumours are constant, but there's nothing confirmed – yet. So, will we ever see or hear from Van Halen again? Who can tell? But history suggests that, with this lot, we should expect the unexpected.

"This tour is like one giant celebration with all the fans that've been there forever," Hagar said at the start of the 2004 tour. "People are really excited about this, and it makes me want to give everything that I've got."

And so, that's the Van Halen story as it stands, right here, right now. The future stretches out in front of them. The past has been full of glories, triumphs and tribulations. But after nearly three decades, they have a new beginning, and a sense of freshness.

Eddie Van Halen has come through so much since he first picked up a guitar all those years ago, and set off on what's been a unique journey. Recently, he was voted the fifth best heavy metal guitarist of all time by *Guitar World* magazine (Black Sabbath's Tony Iommi came top), which proves his enduring influence and popularity – and bear in mind that he is far from being a strictly metal axe attacker.

"I've been at this for over 25 fucking years. I've taken them!" he recently said to former Smashing Pumpkins' mainman Billy Corgan. "There's a plaque on our wall that says we've sold over 65 million albums, and I don't feel I've accomplished anything. I feel like I'm just getting started. Music is for people. The word 'pop' is simply short for popular. It means that people like it. I'm just a normal jerk who happens to make music. As long as my brain and fingers work, I'm cool."

Eddie effectively re-invented the electric guitar - he made it sexy, dynamic and crucial at a time when things were starting to stagnate. Without his impact, it might even have died away. But let's leave the last word to one of the man's greatest admirers, Leslie West of Mountain, a guitar great in his own right:

"I don't think I've ever heard anyone do with a guitar what Eddie has done. Everyone who loves rock music today owes that man a huge debt."

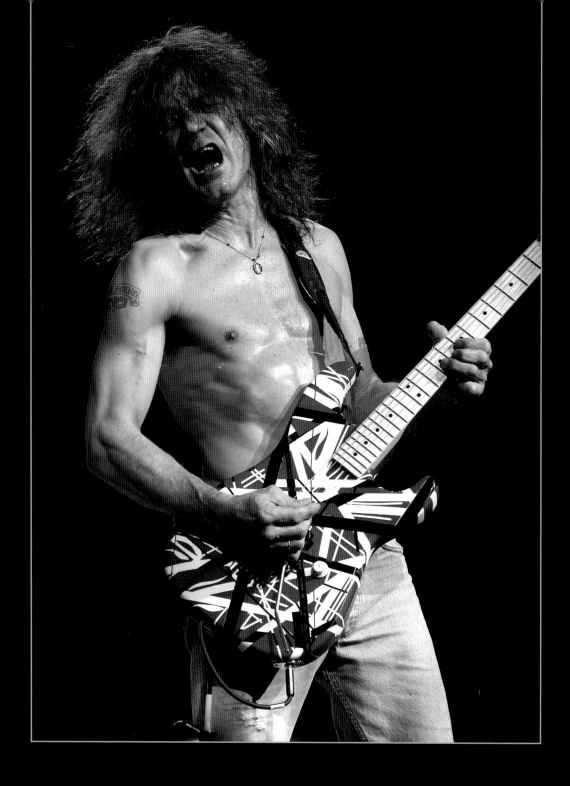

As well as being a supreme player, Eddie Van Halen has always
been an inveterate experimenter with guitars. The modified Fender
Stratocaster above is known as the 'Frankenstrat'. In its various
incarnations, this guitar featured a single humbucker in bridge
position, an unvarnished maple neck and a locking-nut vibrato
system. Eddie generally uses light strings, tuned a semitone down.

Eddie Van Halen

THE MUSIC

EDDIE'S GEAR

Quiet guitars

Eddie's first guitar was a nylon-stringed flamenco model he got when brother Alex gave up guitar for drums and Eddie switched from drums to guitar. Eddie once said he didn't like acoustic guitar because it "wasn't loud enough" so it's no surprise that he soon moved over to electric, his first real instrument being a Japanese Teisco Del Rey four pickup model. Having studied classical piano, violin and music theory, he made fast progress and soon became the worthy owner of several classic instruments. His first serious guitar was a gold-top Gibson Les Paul with 'soap-bar' (P90) pickups. But it is said that he didn't like the way the Les Paul bridge was so high off the body. Palm-muting is an important part of Eddie's technique and the Strat design would suit him more. A Les Paul junior was also an early addition to the collection.

A New Sound

A 1961 Gibson 335 made the sort of sound Eddie was looking for, with its fat hum-cancelling 'PAF' pickups, but the vibrato arm, Gibson's take on the Bigsby design, was hardly the tool for what he had in mind: he describes his dive-bomb whammy-bar antics as "falling off buildings". A 1958 Fender Stratocaster was found to have a vibrato that could do the job, though care was needed to keep the guitar in tune after any big dips with the bar. The single coil pickups were a bit thin sounding, however, and Eddie had ruled out the use of a pre-amp or effects box to thicken the sound. He wanted to play the tubes in the amp rather than the artificial distortion of a fuzz box, which would just cause even more hum from the single coils. A period of experimentation followed, during which Eddie admits that he "butchered" many fine guitars.

First he tried sawing the 335 bridge in half to see whether the vibrato could be made to work only on the top three strings. Eddie hoped that the lower three strings would stay in tune if the vibrato abuse took the top three out, at least enabling him to get to the end of the song. The Gibson vibrato was designed for delicate fluctuations in pitch, (true vibrato, in other words), not the vertiginous dives Eddie had in mind. A better plan was to take a pickup out of the 335 and put it in the vintage Stratocaster. A few hours with a chisel and a soldering iron and the body was routed and the pickup installed, rotated slightly to compensate for the wider string spacing of the Fender's bridge. The Strat's vibrato bridge plate was made to lie flat against the body, preventing any upwards bends, but ensuring that it had a definite point of rest to give some stability to the tuning. When the guitar was ready we can only guess at the young guitarist's excitement as he played it for the first time and, grinning from ear to ear, realised "you can't BUY one of these".

Inventing the SuperStrat

This modified Strat was the first 'SuperStrat', a style of guitar which was to become increasingly popular in the 1980s, with most manufacturers offering their own versions. Some manufacturers (Charvel and Jackson, for example) initially built their entire catalogue around this one type of guitar, combining Strat-type looks with humbucking pickups and a whammy-bar, particularly after the development of the Floyd Rose locking bridge and nut. This first modded guitar is not, however, the one photographed on the cover of the first Van Halen

album, as the body and neck were replaced with parts bought (for $50 and $80) from Wayne Charvel, who had a growing business supplying and fitting custom parts for standard Gibson and Fender guitars. Charvel had no wood shop at the time, so all his necks and bodies were originally made by Boogie Bodies, run by Lynn Ellsworth, a guitar builder and spare parts provider. Eddie painted the unfinished body black and white using Schwinn bicycle paints and a much-copied look was born.

Eddie re-fretted the guitar with large Gibson fret-wire and also removed all the varnish

from the maple neck for a more tactile playing experience. He only installed one pickup, as he had found that optimising the amp for the neck pickup meant sacrificing the sound of the bridge pickup and vice-versa. He decided to go with the bridge pickup alone, using different playing techniques to vary the sound; the neck pickup you can see in photographs of this guitar is not connected. Eddie used light-gauge strings, 009"-042" and usually tuned somewhere in the region of a semi-tone flat, giving a very light set-up to his guitars and making the string tension on his Strat-type guitars more like that found on the shorter scale Gibson Les Paul or 335. This original guitar was used on *Van Halen* in 1978 and all the succeeding albums and tours through to 1984. But Eddie wasn't through with modifying this instrument; over the years he tried it with various combinations of Kramer necks and Floyd Rose vibratos before going over to using complete Kramer guitars. During this time this original 'Frankenstrat' guitar changed colour from black and white to red, black and white.

Destroyer Destroyed

Any tracks on these early albums that did not need the vibrato bar were played on an Ibanez Destroyer (left), which can be seen on the front cover of the *Women and Children First* album. This guitar body was made from Korina, a noted and unusual tonewood, and features a tune-a-matic style bridge with a separate tailpiece, and two pickups; the bridge pickup has been replaced with a PAF. Eddie ruefully admits ruining this guitar for the photo session for the album by cutting a lump of wood from the lower end of the body to make it look more interesting. The resulting loss of mass from the bridge area led him at first to think that he had damaged the pickup, but any number of replacement pickups couldn't cure the fact that what had once been a fat and warm sounding guitar now sounded thin and weedy. He had to borrow another Destroyer to finish the album sessions.

The Floyd solution

Working with the Strat vibrato had always been a problem. When you dip the arm, the string, including the length between nut and tuning head, becomes looser. Because of friction in the nut, that section stays loose when the bar is released, forcing the sounding part of the string to become tighter to compensate and thus sound sharp. Twanging the bar upwards can pull the string through the nut to restore normal tuning but if the alignment of the string around the string-post has changed you may be out of tune till the end of the song. Eddie's solution was to use Schaller tuners and loop the string upwards on the string post, thus minimising downward pressure in the nut. A brass nut with wide grooves also helped, especially when oiled, but strings still tended to go out. Eddie rarely plays bar chords right across the neck, however, and, with the aforementioned upwards pull of the bar he could usually find enough strings in tune to get to the end of the song.

In the early 1980s the Frankenstrat guitar was fitted with a unique vibrato bridge and locking nut hand-made by Seattle-based guitarist/designer Floyd Rose. Floyd had been struggling with the same tuning problems as Eddie, but had an inventor's approach and complementary machining and foundry skills. As an experiment he tried super-gluing the strings in the nut and found that most of the tuning problems were solved. Those that remained, he figured, were down to the bridge. The nut problem was cured on a more permanent basis by installing a 'locking nut', a flat plate to which were bolted, using allen-key bolts, three steel squares each of which clamped a pair of strings immovably in place. The guitar couldn't be tuned without un-clamping the strings, but at least there could be no more slipping through the nut. He then designed a bridge that floated on two knife-edge pivot points instead of the six screws of the Fender, with the strings clamped into the top of the saddles. There was a Fender-style bridge block beneath the bridge plate to which the balancing springs were attached, but as the strings did not pass through the block there was no chance of them moving and affecting the tuning.

Floyd showed his product to Linn Ellsworth, who put him in touch with Eddie Van Halen.

Floyd was later to recall that he had a simple sales pitch; he would push the arm down until the strings were hanging off the neck and then let go and play a chord. Customers were invariably impressed by the stability of the tuning. The original Floyd Rose could not be tuned at all without unclamping but the Floyd Rose II came with fine tuners that could cope with small adjustments. Periodically the player would have to centre these, unclamp the nut and tune using the machine heads, and then re-clamp the nut for further dive-bombing.

Eddie admits to not being too sure about the effect the new bridge had on his tone at first, but the 'Floyd' definitely worked. The inconvenience of the locking nut and the need to summon a mechanic if you broke a string seemed minor problems when compared to the joy of combining unrestricted whammy abuse with stable tuning. This type of bridge became essential kit for all 'SuperStrat' guitars. Eddie continued to prefer the Fender vibrato in the studio, where there was time to re-tune between takes if necessary, but for live work the Floyd couldn't be beaten. Some other noted Floyd-playing guitarists from the 1980s had their bridges set up to be fully-floating, thus allowing some up-bending using the vibrato; Eddie prefers his to be resting on the guitar body. This has certain tonal advantages, and it also keeps the guitar in tune if you break a string. Furthermore, you can rest your hand on the bridge for palm muting without sending the whole guitar out of tune, and can have the springs as tight as you like to stop the bridge tilting up when string bending.

'5150'

The Kramer guitar company had started out in 1976, making guitars with aluminium necks, before heading into the SuperStrat business. By 1982 they were making wood-necked guitars including a one or two humbucker model called the Pacer. The pickups were rear-loaded so the guitar needed no scratch-plate. The Kramer company was also co-operating with Floyd Rose on the development and machining necessary to produce his bridge and nut in large quantities. Eddie Van Halen had been using Kramer necks on his first Frankenstrat for some time and it was inevitable that Kramer would eventually build a guitar for him. Eddie combined a Pacer body with a Kramer neck copied from the one on his old Ibanez Destroyer with a 'hockey stick' or 'banana' style headstock. There was a Floyd Rose vibrato and a single humbucker in the bridge position. The exact origin of the pickup is uncertain but it seems likely to have been a Seymour Duncan '59 that Eddie rewound by hand and wax potted himself.

Eddie also removed all the varnish from the neck and sanded and dressed the frets by hand, not caring that this left the wood stained and dirty. The guitar was finished using cans of spray paint in Eddie's classic red with white and black stripes with the number 5150 (taken from the Los Angeles Police Department code for involuntary psychiatric admission) behind the bridge in reflective stick-on tape. Once again this guitar demonstrates his attention to detail combined with a complete disregard for the cosmetic conventions of guitar building. Bear in mind also that at this point he had already had four million selling albums and was probably a multi-millionaire. In guitar terms could have anything he wanted, and yet he's staying in at nights to put 5,000 turns of copper wire on his own hand-wound pickup.

For the next few years Eddie was an endorser of Kramer guitars and had several other similar guitars built including one with two necks, combining an old aluminium neck from the earlier line of Kramers with a contemporary wooden neck with a 'banana' headstock. Other guitars from this period included a Steinberger which was fitted with a 'Trans-Trem', which allowed chordal bends while staying in tune and which could even be locked in different keys. Trans-Trem units were also fitted to various Kramers and some of the Ernie Ball/Music Man and Peavey guitars that Eddie was to endorse in the future.

Marshall amplifiers

One type of amplifier features prominently on the first eight Van Halen studio albums. It is a Marshall Super Lead 100 watt that Eddie has owned since his early teens. The amp has not been modified in any way, save for the replacement of worn-out components such as transformers, valves and valve seats. Crucial to Eddie's sound, however, is the use of a variac, a voltage control device that he used to reduce the input voltage to around 90 volts from the normal 110, and which would in turn reduce the internal voltage. Running the valves inefficiently, or 'cold' in this way causes them to distort more easily and adds a touch-sensitive element also found in early 'tweed' Fenders which ran on lower voltages than the later 'blackface' models. This sound became known as the 'brown sound' due to its connection with the 'brown-outs' caused by voltage reductions in electricity supplies to major cities.

For live shows six or eight Marshalls could be on stage, though often only two would be in use, with the others as spares in case of component failure. Eddie's amps are run flat-out, allowing the power tubes to generate rich harmonic distortion very different from the buzzy pre-amp distortion made by master volume amplifiers. The amps would need to be re-valved on a weekly basis due to the added wear and tear caused by the variac. In his seminal *Tube Amp Book* Aspen Pitman warns against the use of a variac, because it shortens the life of all the components in the amp; variacs are rightly used by technicians to gradually bring an amp up to its operating voltage whilst checking its symptoms on test equipment. He adds "improper use of variacs is one of the things that keep technicians in business". You have been warned, although clearly this wasn't a problem for Eddie!

In the studio, Eddie credits engineer Don Landee with responsibility for his recorded sound, though a simple set-up of two Shure SM57 mics on a single Marshall 4x12 cabinet was the most common means of getting Eddie's notes to tape. Both live and in the studio, Eddie used the simplest of effects. At this time there was a general move by the top players towards effect racks, midi-controlled switching and elaborate stage boxes. Eddie stuck with a battery powered MXR Phase 90 and Flanger, a Univox echo box and two Maestro Echoplexes, the latter being mounted in 'the bomb', an empty shell from World War 2 designed for target practice. A Roland Space Echo supplies chorus sounds for 'Little Guitars' on *Diver Down*.

Music Man

In 1984 Leo Fender's Music Man company was bought by Ernie Ball, best known at the time for guitar strings. The company became known as Ernie Ball Music Man and gradually began to extend its guitar range, usually with instruments that remained true to the Fender legacy. In 1991 they launched the Edward Van Halen guitar, the result of a collaboration between

Eddie and the technicians at Music Man and DiMarzio, the pickup manufacturer. This guitar (left) was the first production instrument to bear Eddie's name, one that he was involved in from the start and that was intended to meet his specifications from headstock to strap button.

The 'do-it-yourself' appearance of Eddie's guitars was gone for ever. The instrument had a bound body of basswood with a quilted maple top and is shaped like a cross between a Les Paul and a Telecaster. The one-piece maple neck and fingerboard have 22 frets and an oiled finish and the guitar comes with a pair of special DiMarzio pickups. Guitars with two pickups often have the same model in both positions; Eddie worked with DiMarzio to design a differently voiced front pickup that works with the rear, getting round the earlier problem of mismatching for a given amp setting. There is no scratch-plate; the pickups are screwed directly to the body to enable them to pick up the resonance of the wood. A Floyd Rose vibrato made by Gotoh is supplied flat to the body, balanced by the distinctive Music Man four against two tuner arrangement on the headstock. There is just one volume knob, eccentrically labelled 'tone', no tone control, and the pickup selector is below the front pickup near the front horn. The neck re-creates the profile one of Ed's earlier Kramer guitars and is slightly asymmetrical. Even from new these guitars feel worn-in and comfortable and are superb instruments, suitable for a wide range of playing styles.

Peavey 5150

The album *For Unlawful Carnal Knowledge* was the first to feature the new guitar, and it also marked a new departure for Eddie in amplification terms. He had felt that the old Marshall was starting to fade, and experimented with a Soldano SLO-100 whilst working with Peavey on the development of an amplifier to endorse. The prototype arrived at Eddie's 5150 studio towards the end of the album's over dubbing sessions, though sources close to the band pointed out that it didn't seem to matter which amp he played through, Eddie always sounded like Eddie.

The new amp was christened the Peavey 5150 and came with matching 4X12 speaker cabinet. Essentially a cross between the Marshall and the Soldano, it was a footswitchable two channel (rhythm and lead) amp with an output of 120 watts from four 6L6 valves, in contrast to the Marshall's EL34s. The EQ section is shared between the two channels, but a later Mark II version added bright and crunch switches on an improved clean channel with separate channel EQs. There is also a 5150 combo version of this amp, with 2X12 speakers in a sealed cabinet and 60w output. The album *Balance* was 75 per cent Peavey 5150, with the rest of the amplification duties going to Marshalls.

Peavey Wolfgang

The Peavey company were keen to exploit their successful collaboration with Eddie and in 1996 persuaded him to begin endorsing a new guitar. Eddie severed his connection with Music Man, who re-branded his EVH guitar as the Music Man Axis; the new guitar was named the Peavey Wolfgang after Eddie's son. The Wolfgang (overleaf) echoes most of the essential elements of the Music Man. The shape of the headstock was changed to accommodate three-a-side tuners and the body lengthened slightly, with the addition of a sharper top cutaway. The pickup switch was moved to the top horn, wired in reverse so that 'up' selects the bridge pickup, and a tone control was added. The Floyd Rose vibrato was flat to the body and included an ingenious 'D-Tuner' that can instantly drop the bottom string a whole tone. This device would be unusable on a guitar with a floating bridge as the other strings would go out of tune.

The Return of Frankenstrat

When Eddie and the band returned to touring in 2004 he was still using the Peavey Wolfgang, but a new endorsement was on the way. Eddie had been working with Charvel on the 'EVH Art Series', a range of guitars echoing his original Frankenstrat design with re-creations of three classic Van Halen striped finishes: red/black/white, white/black, and black/yellow. These guitars have a basswood body with a Fender-style bolt-on 22-fret maple neck with an oiled finish. The fingerboard is also maple and there is a single humbucking pickup and a Floyd Rose vibrato. Only the white/black model has a scratch plate. Eddie formally ended his relationship with the Peavey company in December 2004 (after 13 years). As Eddie owns the rights to the '5150' and 'Wolfgang' names, Peavey has renamed the 5150 amp the 6505, commemorating its fortieth year in business (1965 – 2005). A new guitar, named the HP Special after Peavey owner and founder Hartley Peavey, will replace the Wolfgang.

Taking the long view of Eddie's adventures in guitars and amps, he seems eccentric, contrary, and at times comical. But the truth is he has an exceptionally clear idea of what he wants to hear and play, and everything else becomes irrelevant. Combine this with his sense of humour and you have upside-down switches, 'volume' labelled 'tone' and some of the cosmetic shortcomings of his 'homemade' instruments, including unconnected pickups, unfinished necks and cheap paint jobs. Eddie introduced the guitar world to a whole range of playing techniques and invented the instrument necessary for playing them. He set the style that everyone followed for the next decade and re-defined rock guitar. When Eddie talks about his music he often repeats that the sound and feel are the most important things to him; it's not so surprising that these two elements have led him to develop his own style in guitars and amplifiers with a healthy disregard for convention.

PLAY LIKE EDDIE

Grooves and riffs

As Eddie squawked, squealed and dive-bombed his way to fame back in 1978, some of the most important things about his playing were overlooked. While everyone noticed the flashy guitar pyrotechnics, many listeners failed to appreciate his style, taste and humour. He was also a great rhythm player, and had the benefit of playing with one of the best rock rhythm sections of all time. Whatever you do with this book, don't overlook Eddie's rhythm parts just to concentrate on the widdly bits! In many ways tight rhythm playing is more important to getting a gig than being able to 'shred'. Tunes like 'Runnin' With The Devil', 'Ain't Talkin' 'Bout Love', 'Unchained' and 'Hot For Teacher' are studies in nailing a groove and locking with the rhythm section.

In the coming pages we'll look at these tracks and others to try to learn lessons that we can apply to our own playing. Listen to the CD tracks, look closely at the exercises and practise playing along with the backing tracks. These parts are not technically all that hard, so this is the place to start building your ability. Although Eddie nearly always tuned his guitar a semitone flat, I've opted here to remain at standard tuning, so you can be ready to go without needing to retune.

Eddie rarely used bar (or barre) chords, meaning the type that involve using your first finger across all six strings. Bar chords make a big fat sound that doesn't always sit well in the mix as it leaves so little room for anything else. Many of Eddie's rhythm parts rely instead

FIGURE 1: three C major inversions

C E G	E G C	G C E
root position	first inversion	second inversion
(root in bass)	(third in bass)	(fifth in bass)

FIGURE 2: C major inversions on the top 3 strings

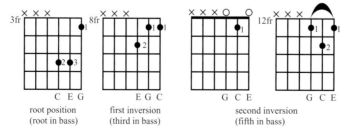

C E G	E G C	G C E	G C E
root position	first inversion	second inversion	
(root in bass)	(third in bass)	(fifth in bass)	

on 'triads'; three note chords played, in this case, mostly on the D, G, and B strings of the guitar. Figure 1 shows three versions of a C major triad. Each chord shape consists of the root (C), the third (E), and the fifth (G). Just to be complete, Figure 2 shows the same inversions shifted across to the top three strings.

Exercise 1 (CD tracks 2 and 3) shows how Eddie might use shapes like these to create a rhythm part over a fixed repeated bass note, also called a 'pedal' note. You can hear this sort of approach in tunes like 'Runnin' With The Devil'. The *xxx* signs are muted strings; they can make a big difference to any rhythm guitar part. Lay your left-hand index finger lightly across the five highest strings around the seventh fret as you strum a quick up-and-down stroke.

Adding one finger to the second inversion shape creates a 'sus' or 'sus4' chord (Figure 3). What's happening here is that the third of the chord (E) is being raised or 'suspended' one fret to become the fourth (F). The musical effect is that the raised note seems to want to go back to where it came from, to resolve the tension of the 'sus' chord.

EXERCISE 1: rhythm using triads CD TRACK 2 / CD TRACK 3 (drum and bass backing track)

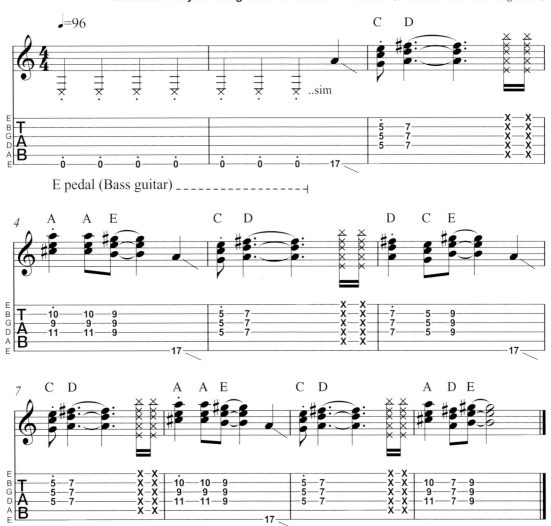

FIGURE 3: major and 'sus4' chords

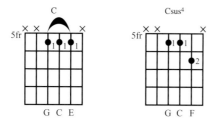

Exercise 2 (CD tracks 4 and 5) is an example of a rhythm part built from alternating major and sus4 chords. You can hear this sort of playing on 'Unchained' from *Fair Warning*. On the original the guitar is in 'Drop D' tuning, where the low E string is taken down a whole tone to D, and the song is in the key of D. Here I've kept to standard tuning and played in E. Notice how the rhythm is 'pushed', coming in before the first beat, but returns to the downbeat half way through. This sort of rhythmic shift adds drive and lets you play the riff twice without sounding repetitive.

Exercises 1 and 2 would be good for intros and choruses, but for a verse you'd need something a little more restrained; Eddie often uses an open A major chord, sometimes reduced to just root and fifth, when it's called A5 (Figure 4).

EXERCISE 2: rhythm using triads and sus chords **CD track 4 / CD track 5** (backing track)

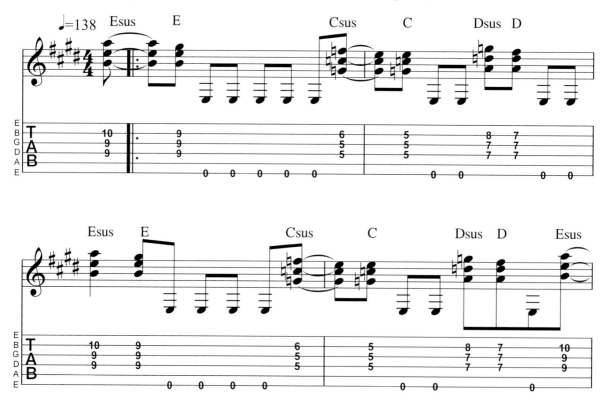

EXERCISE 2 continued

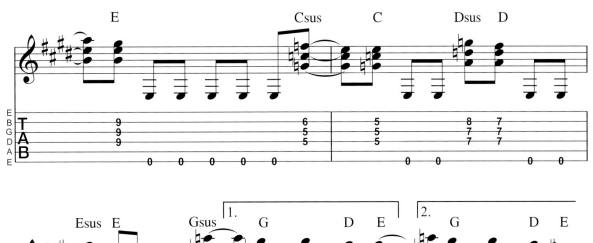

FIGURE 4: A major triad and A5 chord

 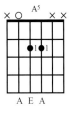

Exercise 3 (CD tracks 6 and 7) is an example of Eddie's playing using this chord shape and some of the other notes that fit around it. 'Runnin' With The Devil' and 'You Really Got Me' are good examples of this approach.

Notice that some notes are allowed to ring on and some are palm-muted. Place the outside edge of your pick hand on the strings just in front of the bridge while you're picking. You can move it back and forth to vary the amount of muting; there really is this much detail in Eddie's playing. Something like this would make a great verse to go with a chorus like CD track 2.

EXERCISE 3: A5 rhythm CD track 6 / CD track 7 (backing track)

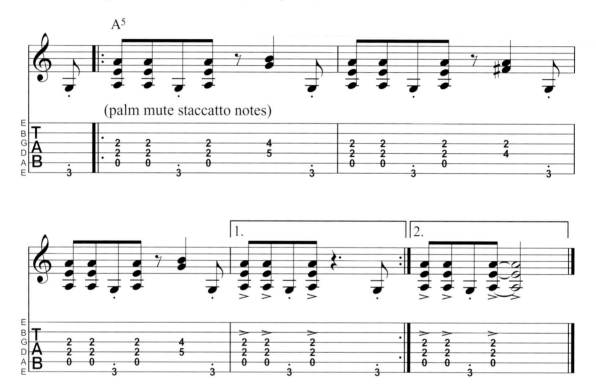

In addition to triads, Eddie often uses arpeggios to create his rhythm parts. An arpeggio is simply a chord played one note at a time. **Exercise 4** (CD track 8) is an example, based around the chords of A minor, F major and G major. Figure 5 shows you the shapes.

The F chord needs a short bar covering two strings with your first finger. For the G chord, mute the A string with the underside of the third finger while it holds down the sixth string and mute the top E with the underside of your hand. These fingerings would let you strum the chords as well as play them as arpeggios.

The exercise shows how breaking up these chords creates rhythmic tension that drives the song forward, helped out by the palm muting. 'Ain't Talkin' 'Bout Love', on the first Van Halen album, is a good example of this sort of playing.

EXERCISE 4: arpeggios CD track 8

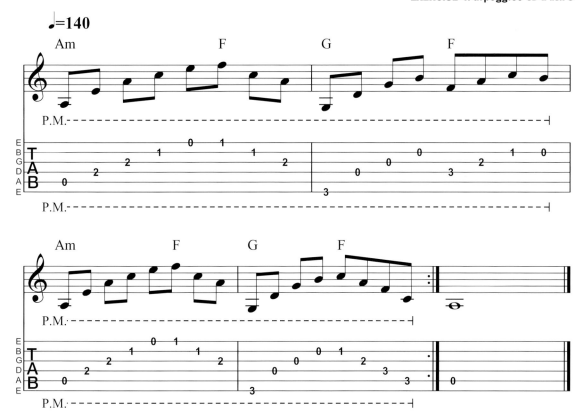

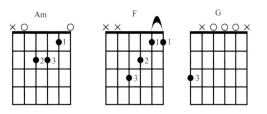

FIGURE 5: Am, F and G chords

Adding a single-note riff to an intro like that in Exercise 4 will create interest and allow you to re-use it later in the song, maybe as a verse. **Exercise 5** (CD track 9) is the same opening, but this time with a riff added, using pinched harmonics. I'll explain these later. Again, 'Ain't Talkin' 'Bout Love' inspired this track.

EXERCISE 5: arpeggios and riffs CD track 9

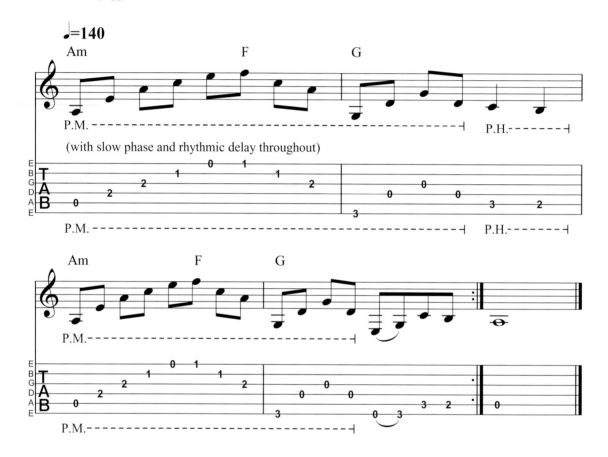

Exercise 6 (CD track 10): the same arpeggio approach sounds good mixed in with the five chords from Exercise 3, as heard on CD track 6.

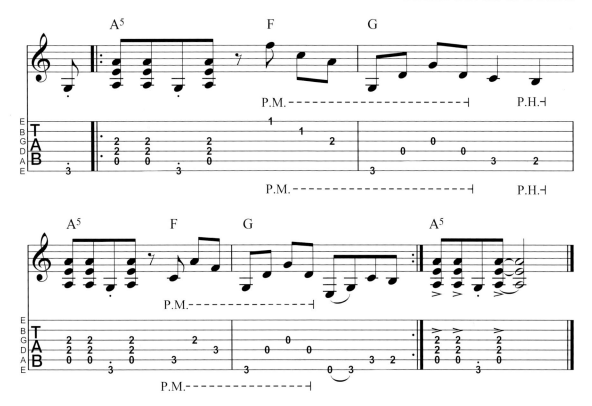

The final example from this tour of Eddie's rhythm playing, **Exercise 7** (CD tracks 11 and 12), ties up any loose ends by including all the styles discussed so far and throwing in a few pull-offs, hammer-ons and slides in the way that you'll hear on a tune like 'Hot For Teacher'.

EXERCISE 7 CD track 11 / CD track 12 (backing track)

Fills and thrills

In this section we're going to be looking at everything that comes under the heading of lead guitar, but we're going to be starting with 'fills', before moving on to soloing ideas.

A 'fill' is a convenient term for any bits of guitar-playing that fill up the gaps between the vocal lines. They form only a small part of his overall output, but Eddie's fills are some of the most characteristic and quirky elements of his playing. For **Exercise 8** (CD track 13), let's start off with a two-fingered trill like he plays in 'Runnin' with the Devil' at around 1:28. Stop two strings with your first finger at the seventh fret and then quickly hammer-on and pull-off with the third and fourth fingers at the ninth fret.

EXERCISE 8: two-string slurs **CD track 13**

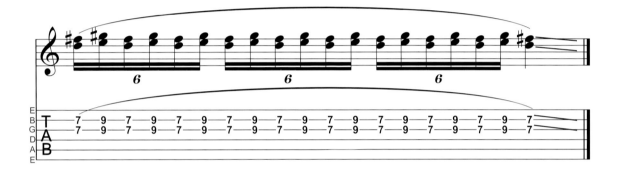

Fills using natural harmonics

Natural harmonics are made by touching a string lightly over certain frets; picking near the bridge helps to bring them out, as does the compressing effect of cranking up the amp or using a distortion pedal. They'll ring on longer if you release the finger pressure once you've picked. Basically they are found at the 12th, seventh, fifth and fourth frets; the fourth fret harmonic is also found at the ninth fret and these positions can be mirrored above the 12th fret. Try thinking in terms of distance rather than fret numbers and you'll get the hang of it. For example, the fifth fret harmonic can also be found over the 24th fret (or where it would be if your guitar doesn't have one!). Other, weaker harmonics can be found just in front of the third fret, about halfway between the second and third frets and more or less over the second fret. Again, these will pop out clearly if you've got some distortion running.

This technique can be used to produce a whole range of strange pitches and sounds, because harmonics happen all over the guitar. Crank your amp up and slide your finger lightly along a string as you pick and it will produce all sorts of harmonic squawks and squeals. Have a listen to these two exercises on the CD. **Exercise 9** (CD track 14) shows the most prominent harmonics on the 6th string.

Exercise 10 (CD track 15) is a fill which uses harmonics like those in 'Runnin' With The Devil'.

EXERCISE 9: harmonics at frets 12, 7, 5, 4, in front of 3, behind 3, and 2. **CD track 14**

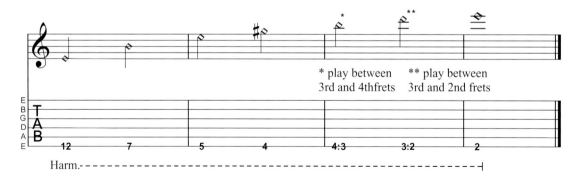

* play between   ** play between
3rd and 4thfrets   3rd and 2nd frets

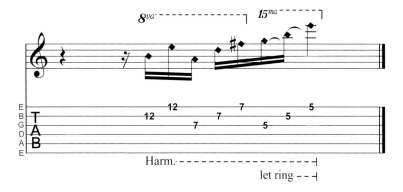

'Artificial' and 'tapped' harmonics

All the natural harmonics are available on fretted notes too. You just have count up the right number of frets above the note you're holding down. So if you're holding a note at the second fret you'll find harmonics at the 14th, ninth, seventh, etc. You have to use your right hand to sound them though; one way is to hold the pick between your thumb and middle finger (which is how Eddie holds it) and touch the harmonic point with your index finger while picking. This would be called an 'artificial' harmonic, marked in the music by the sign 'A.H.' Eddie came up with another way, however, which is to tap the string over the harmonic with the index finger. You can hear this trick at the beginning of 'Spanish Fly', and in **Exercise 11** (CD track 16); hold down a G bar chord at the third fret and tap harmonics around the 15th, tenth and eighth frets.

EXERCISE 11: tapped harmonics on a held G chord CD track 16

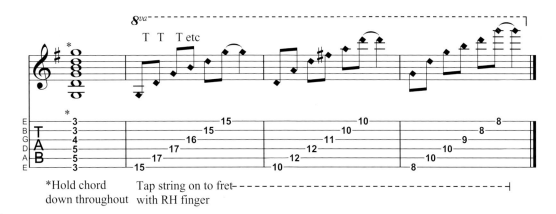

Moving on to some of the ideas found in Eddie's solos, you can then tap a harmonic on any note, and use bends too. **Exercise 12** (CD track 17) starts with a bend on the 5th fret, G string, then you tap the harmonic 12 frets up (the 17th fret) and release the bend. Continue bending, tapping and releasing as instructed in the tab. It's really a blues-flavoured lick with a modern twist.

EXERCISE 12: bending and tapping harmonics CD track 17

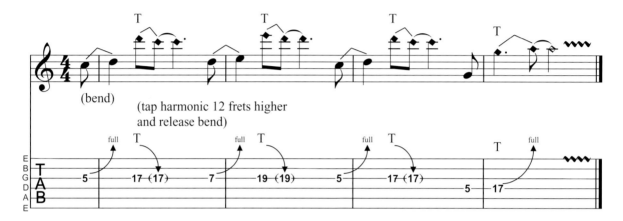

'Pinched' harmonics

These are a little more difficult both to do and to explain, but add a lot of character to your playing if you can get them together. The trick is to touch the string with the side of your picking-hand thumb as you pick; you're doing the same sort of thing as when you play artificial harmonics but the thumb does the necessary 'touching' bit. The result is a note that combines some of the normal, or 'fundamental', pitch with an amount of the harmonic too. Some people say the 'P.H.' sign used actually stands for 'partial harmonic'. You choose!

You can hear this technique in the rhythm part at the start of 'Ain't Talkin' 'Bout Love'. The hard thing is to know where to find the harmonics, as their positions change as you move your left hand around the guitar. As a rough guide start halfway between the end of the fingerboard and the bridge and you'll find there are more as you move your picking hand nearer the bridge. **Exercise 13** (CD track 18) demonstrates this in another blues-based lick.

EXERCISE 13: 'pinched' harmonics **CD track 18**

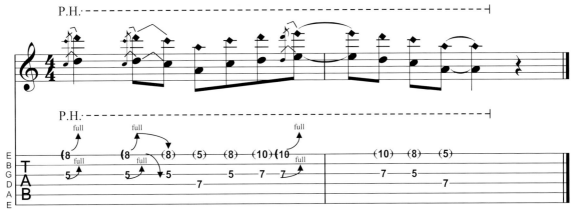

(approx sounding pitches shown in brackets)

Tapping

If you can tap a harmonic it figures that you can tap and hold any string against the fret and it could sound just like you picked it. Many guitarists have used pull-offs between fretted notes and open strings but Eddie was definitely the first to get his right hand in on the act and play some jaw-droppingly fast arpeggios using combinations of tapped right-hand notes and hammer-ons and pull-offs. If you don't include open strings then you have a pattern that can be moved around the neck. 'Eruption' and 'Spanish Fly' both use this technique. It's said that in the early days Eddie turned his back on the audience while using it, to avoid being copied; it has now become a staple and accepted way of playing both electric and acoustic guitar.

Exercise 14 (CD track 19) uses some of those fast arpeggios in a classic bit of two-hand tapping like the intro to 'Hot For Teacher'. Essentially it's a four-note minor arpeggio built on the open string. By moving the middle two notes up a tone (two frets) you get a major arpeggio with the fifth fret note as its root. Tap and pull-off with your right-hand index or middle finger on the note at the 12th fret; all the other notes are hammered-on or pulled-off with the left hand. As you can see, you can play it on any string you like. It's going to require a lot of co-ordination between the right 'tapping' hand and the left 'hammer-on and pull-off' hand to get it fast and smooth, and you'd better be able to stretch your left hand from the third fret to the seventh fret. Take it slowly at first, relax, and don't struggle!

This exercise ends with a lick showing how Eddie uses his right hand to add notes to fast scale passages. This one looks a bit like a blues scale but is really a finger pattern; we'll come back to finger patterns later.

EXERCISE 14: tapping arpeggios CD track 19

Tapping chord shapes

Later on in his career, Eddie got into tapping chord shapes using the fingers of both hands on the neck at once. This example (**Exercise 15**, CD track 20) should give you the idea. It is based on an idea in the lead-in to the solo on 'Judgement Day' (*For Unlawful Carnal Knowledge*) should give you the idea. Eddie sticks to one shape moved up the neck, but here we're outlining three shapes of a G7 chord , tapping with the first and second fingers of both hands.

Eddie plays this sort of figure with his left hand coming over the neck, rather than the usual position. This has the advantage of allowing him to use the outside of his left hand to damp the open strings. He 'palms' his pick while doing this, holding it between the curled right-hand fingers he's not using. Other players put it between their teeth! See which suits you best.

EXERCISE 15: chordal tapping CD track 20

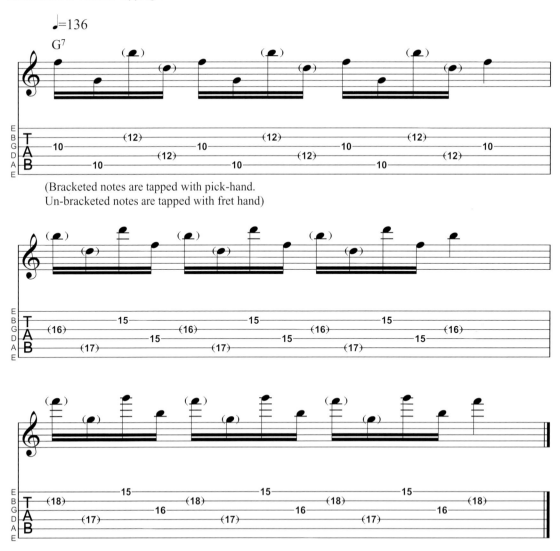

(Bracketed notes are tapped with pick-hand.
Un-bracketed notes are tapped with fret hand)

Not everything Eddie does is unconventional; we've already seen that left-hand trills are an important part of his armoury, as they were for players like Hendrix and Clapton. Using the right hand on the neck can give you some unusual options, however, as is shown by **Exercise 16** (CD track 21), which combines a right-hand tap with a slide like one in 'You Really Got Me' (*Van Halen*). It starts with some rapid trills from the fret hand, then you tap and slide two frets with your pick-hand finger and pull off back to the trills.

EXERCISE 16: tap and slide CD track 21

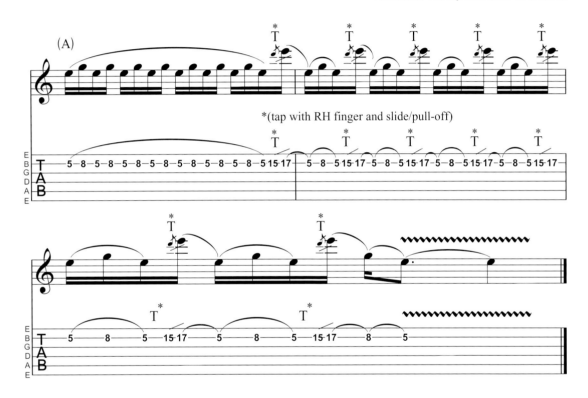

The vibrato bar

Leo Fender's marketing people have a lot to answer for, because they described the Fender Stratocaster's bridge as having a 'tremolo' device. In fact, tremolo is a regular fluctuation in volume, not pitch. So it should be called a 'vibrato', and as you've seen, that's the term I've tried to stick to here. It has to be said, however, that what Eddie did with the bar hardly comes under the heading of vibrato – perhaps the 1980s term 'whammy bar' would be more appropriate. Huge numbers of guitars today are sold with vibrato bridges, but unless you have a Floyd Rose or a Wilkinson or something similar you may be in for the sort of tuning problems that Eddie found so frustrating in the early days. Remember that Eddie recorded the first few albums using a standard Strat tremolo (vibrato) and check out the chapter on Eddie's Gear to see how to set up and work with the bar to stay in tune.

Eddie uses the vibrato bar to great effect in 'Ain't Talkin' 'Bout Love'. **Exercise 17** (CD track 22) is a phrase inspired by one of his fills. Pick the first note and dip and release the bar, then slide the fret-hand finger, co-ordinating the dipping and releasing of the bar with each new note. You only pick the first note of the phrase, so it's like using the bar instead of the pick.

EXERCISE 17: scoop and slide **CD track 22**

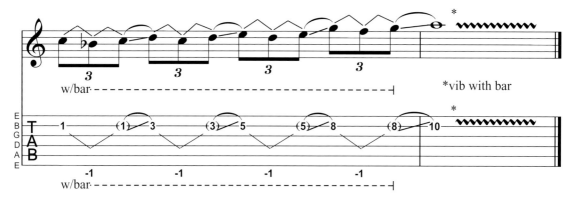

There's so much more that can be done with the bar that it's hard to know where to begin. The obvious thing is to whack an open string and plummet all the way down to Hades. Here's an idea while you're down there. Tap with your left hand to sound any note and hold it down while you let the bar come back up. You should get a big upwards bend. Eddie sets up his vibrato so that it's resting on the body, so upwards bends have to be preceded by dipping the bar down, then releasing it. Many modern Floyd Rose equipped guitars have a routed area behind the bridge which allows considerable scope for up-bends with the bar. Eddie's objection to this is mainly on grounds on tone, as he argues that contact between all the essential elements of the guitar (including the pick-ups, which are screwed directly into the wood rather than being mounted in plastic surrounds) gives a richer sound with more sustain.

Exercise 18 (CD track 23) gets you using your ear to dip the bar 'in tune' so you're hitting exact pitches with it. Tap the sixth string against the fifth fret with a left hand finger to sound the note A and then pull-off to sound the open E string. Let it ring and dip the bar right down until it reaches the A below. Hold it for a moment before tapping the fifth fret again and release the bar slowly, listening as you hear a whole octave bend back up to the A you started with. The track ends with a completely gratuitous (but fun) squealing double-harmonic bend.

EXERCISE 18: tapping and releasing the bar CD track 23

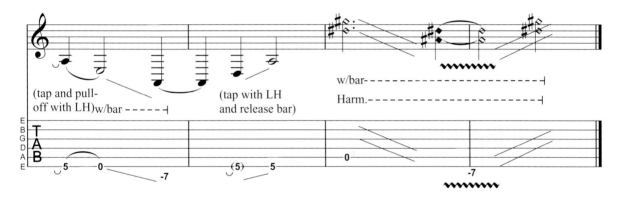

Eddie's Effects

Eddie used simple, but good-sounding effects boxes in the early days, consisting of a flanger and phaser made by MXR, and Univox and Echoplex echo devices. These were later replaced by the very high-tech Eventide Harmonizer, a programmable multi-effect unit in a rack-mountable box. Notice that he often switches an effect on for just one section of a song or solo, using flanging or phasing to add movement to a sequence of arpeggios, or the Echoplex to add interest as a note decays. An exception to this is 'Cathedral' from the album *Diver Down*, which relies on a rhythmic delay effect for the main part of song. Here's how to replicate this effect using your own digital delay.

Set up a 375-millisecond delay and adjust the feedback so that you hear just two repeats of any note you play; around 15-20 per cent feedback works fine. Now get a metronome or a drum machine to give you a click, four beats to the bar at 120 beats per minute and play **Exercise 19** (CD track 24).

What you should be hearing is **Exercise 20** (CD track 25).

EXERCISE 19: double delay CD track 24

(Bracketed notes are sounded by delay unit)

You are playing notes on the eighth-note beat but the delay effect bounces them back on the sixteenth-note beats, making it sound like you're playing twice as fast as you are! I've left out the second delayed note in the tab at certain points for reasons of clarity; it's the first note that's most important for the overall effect. Eddie plays this by tapping with his left hand, coordinating with his right hand on the volume control to produce a slight swell on each note.

Scales and Modes

No examination of Eddie's style would be complete without checking out his choice of notes. In interviews Eddie is dismissive of the sort of analysis that talks about this mode here and that scale there; he keeps coming back to the idea that feel is the most important thing to him. That's not much help to the novice with a neck full of notes and no idea what to play, however. Eddie's approach could be described as 'beyond blues', in that while blues scale notes feature in his playing, and there's a healthy dose of blues vibe and groove about him, he tends to extend the basic five-note minor pentatonic.

The next example, **Exercise 21** (CD track 26), shows the minor pentatonic followed by the blues scale with its flattened fifth (or sharpened fourth) and an added major sixth. The major pentatonic scale is then played in its normal form before being extended in a similar way.

EXERCISE 21: descending minor pentatonic and ascending major pentatonic CD track 26

They are followed by **Exercise 22** (CD track 27), based on a line from 'Eruption' that shows the blues scale with some of the notes you can add in.

Notice the pinched harmonics, which provide the squawks and squeaks and are so much a part of Eddie's style.

Exercise 23 (CD track 28) is the same trick done with a major pentatonic; this is based on a fill from 'You Really Got Me'.

EXERCISE 22: extending the blues scale CD track 27

EXERCISE 23: Extending the Major Pentatonic CD track 28

Modes

Hold on to your seat, we're about to get technical. If you add the second degree to a minor pentatonic scale (the note B in the key of A minor) you almost have a fully-fledged minor scale, as used for the solos in 'Ain't Talkin' 'Bout Love'. Add in the major sixth (F#) and you have the Dorian mode. Put in the minor sixth (F natural) instead and you have the Aeolian mode. Both these are good for playing over A minor chords.

Now take the Dorian and make the minor third (C) into a major third (C#) and you have the Mixolydian Mode. This sounds good over major chords and dominant seventh chords (A7 in this case).

Have a listen to these modes on the CD; see if you can hear the 'minor' flavour of the Dorian, with the slightly darker, more 'gothic' Aeolian, and the more 'major' flavour of the Mixolydian. Examples of these can be found all over Eddie's playing, but as we've already seen he's just as likely to use a finger pattern which sounds good and just happens to look like a scale or mode. **Exercise 24** (CD track 29) gives you all three modes written out.

EXERCISE 24: Dorian, Aeolian and Mixolydian modes CD track 29

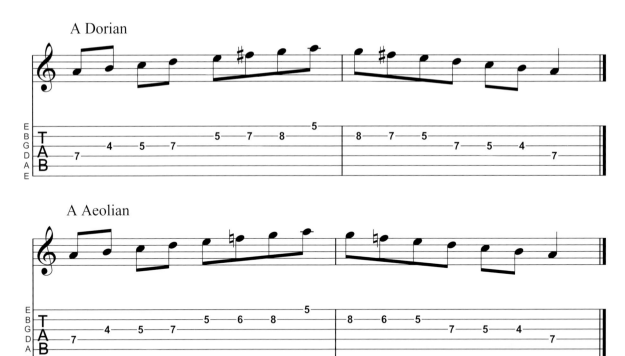

EXERCISE 24: continued

A Mixolydian

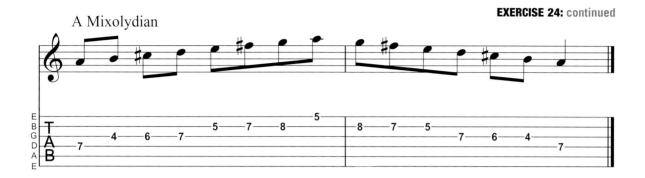

Which brings us to our next example, **Exercise 25** overleaf (CD track 30), which strings together many ideas used in fills to make one of the crazy, off the wall solos that Eddie plays on tracks like 'I'm the One' (*Van Halen*) or 'You're No Good' (*Van Halen II*). We kick off with some triads (like those in Exercise 1) played here using the volume control of the guitar to create a fade-in or 'swell' effect. Then it's on to some fast single note runs. Bars five and six of this track make use of a finger pattern, using fingers one, two and four back-and-forth on adjacent strings. Most of the notes come from a G major scale, but as we're playing in A it could be better described as A Dorian, though the C sharps don't belong. Then the pattern carries on to the second and first strings and you can see that the notes don't fit any of these scales and it's not really a scale at all. Eddie admits to being able to get away with all kinds of so-called 'wrong' notes if he can play fast enough. This kind of playing is called *legato*, from the Italian word for 'joined-up'. Notice that in fast legato passages you can tap 'from nowhere' with your left hand and it sounds like you picked the note.

The legato section ends with harmonics, before moving on to a tricky left-hand pull-off pattern in bar eight. In the following bars we cover octaves played with the vibrato bar (bar nine) and holding a note and bending another up to the same pitch (or 'unison bends') in bar ten. We then move on to fast descending three-note arpeggios in the style of 'Eruption' before returning to finger patterns, this time with palm muting. The climax of the solo is provided by 'tremolo picking', which is extremely fast alternate picking, and a fast two-hand tapping riff between the 12th, seventh and fifth frets. Really this exercise is just a collection of fills, tricks and sounds, but rock guitar solos before Eddie tended to be based on the blues approach of call and response and balanced phrases. After Eddie, anything goes! An extended version of this backing track is included at the end of the CD so you can use it to work on your own ideas.

EXERCISE 25: soloing techniques **CD Track 30**

EXERCISE 25: continued

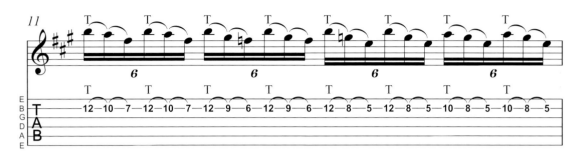

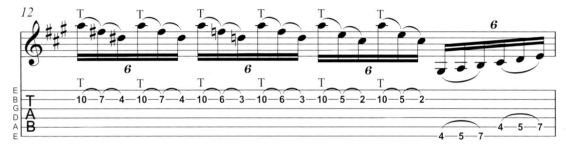

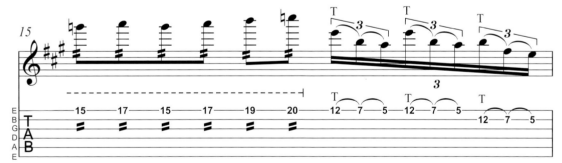

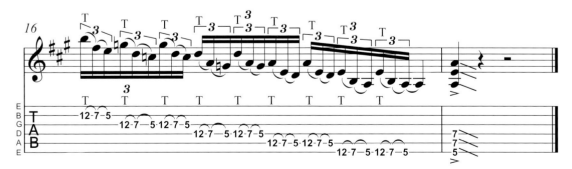

This is a good time to mention that if you listen closely to Eddie's playing you'll hear that many of the pattern-based things he plays are not strictly logical; though there's an underlying pattern, he does not stick to it rigidly, and if things don't turn out right he crams the notes in as needed and uses his ear to come out on the beat. Eddie describes this as "falling down stairs and landing on your feet".

There's a huge range to Eddie's guitar playing. He is a guitar genius who transformed rock guitar playing forever, and within this book there are enough ideas to get you started, not just on copping his style, but on forging your own ideas based on what you can learn from "the most influential American guitarist since Hendrix". Let's give Eddie the last word and end with **Exercise 26** (CD track 31), a riff based on the intro to 'Mean Streets' from *Fair Warning*. It's Eddie at his most innovative, using a funky technique similar to the thumb slaps of bass players. Slap the low E-string with the side of your pick-hand thumb and then tap at the 12th fret with your index finger. Meanwhile your fret hand alternately slaps and mutes the E-string just in front of the nut. This is followed by a passage using right and left hand tapping and tapped harmonics. You'll see that this goes beyond tapping the octave harmonic to include the other notes in the harmonic series. Once you've mastered this, try to come up with your own new sounds and ideas. CD track 32 is an extended backing track in A to help you experiment.

EXERCISE 26: thumb slap and tapping CD track 31

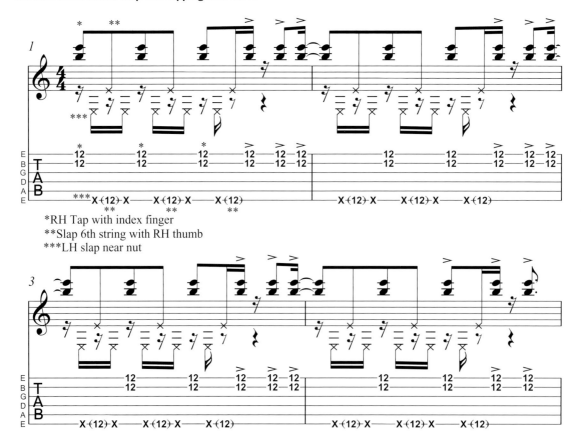

*RH Tap with index finger
**Slap 6th string with RH thumb
***LH slap near nut

*Tap and p.o. with RH

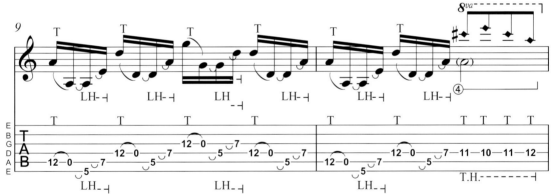

*hold 7th fret A and
tap harm. w. RH

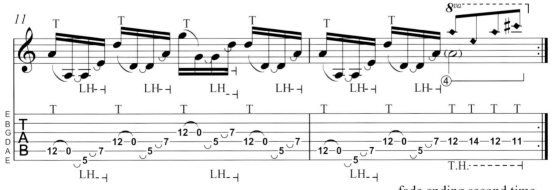

fade ending second time...

CD TRACK LISTING

TRACK 1   Tuning notes EADGBE.

TRACK 2   Rhythm using triads.

TRACK 3   Rhythm using triads backing track.

TRACK 4   Rhythm using triads and sus chords.

TRACK 5   Rhythm using triads and sus chords

backing track.

TRACK 6   Rhythm using 5 chords.

TRACK 7   Rhythm using 5 chords backing track.

TRACK 8   Am G F chord arpeggios.

TRACK 9   Arpeggios and riffs.

TRACK 10   A5 and riff.

TRACK 11   Hot for rhythm.

TRACK 12   Hot for rhythm (backing track).

TRACK 13   Two string slurs.

TRACK 14   Harmonics at frets 12,7, 5,4, in front of 3,

behind 3 and 2nd.

TRACK 15   Harmonic fills.

TRACK 16   Tapped harmonics on a held G chord.

TRACK 17   Bending and tapping harmonics.

TRACK 18   'Pinched' harmonics.

TRACK 19   Tapping arpeggios.

TRACK 20   Chordal tapping.

TRACK 21   Tap and slide.

TRACK 22   Scoop & slide.

TRACK 23   Tapping and releasing the bar.

TRACK 24   Double delay.

TRACK 25   Double double delay.

TRACK 26   Descending minor pentatonic and

ascending major pentatonic.

TRACK 27   Extending the blues scale.

TRACK 28   Extending the major pentatonic.

TRACK 29   Dorian, Aeolian and Mixolydian modes.

TRACK 30   Soloing techniques.

TRACK 31   Thumb slap and tapping.

TRACK 32   Extended backing track in A.

INDEX

ACKNOWLEDGEMENTS

Websites

The official Van Halen website is at www.van-halen.com, whereas www.vanhalen.com is an unofficial fan site. Beyond that there are dozens of fan sites and online traders. There's a news desk at www.vhnd.com, a 'links' site at www.vhlinks.com, and a list of bootlegs of live gigs at www.vhboots.com. For a book called the *Van Halen Encyclopedia* visit www.vanhalenencyclopedia.com, and to buy a t-shirt and other merchandise try www.vanhalenstore.com. Guitar fans might like www.wolfgangregistry.com, www.evh-guitars.com or www.charvel.com. A great site for guitarists generally is www.mikesguitarsite.co.uk. The last time I searched on Google for Van Halen I got 2.3 million hits!

Magazines

Guitar magazines were an essential part of the preparation of this book, with interviews and articles from the following providing much needed factual information.
Thanks to the following:
Guitar World
Guitar Player
Guitar Legends
Guitarist (U.K.)

People

MALCOLM DOME would like to thank *TotalRock*, *Metal Hammer*, *Classic Rock*, *Kerrang!*, www.van-halen.com and The Crobar. And, of course, every member of Van Halen over the years for their musical inspiration. Not to mention the man himself – a true one-off.

ROD FOGG would like to thank Chris Hunt for the loan of vital magazines from his excellent collection, and Matt Cox for the loan of his Peavey Wolfgang. Succinct advice and pithy comment were gratefully received from many sources, especially Huw Price, Bill Puplett, Charlie Chandler and Chandler's Guitars, of Kew, London. My editor, John Morrish, also deserves the highest accolade for his patience and good humour. If you should be here and I've missed you off this list, please accept my thanks and apologies.